The Empire State Building

By the same author

Backgammon: The Action Game
The Waldorf Astoria Cookbook
Europe: A Second Time Around
The Colony Cookbook
Fifth Avenue

Theodore James, Jr.

THE EMPIRE STATE BUILDING

Harper & Row, Publishers · New York · Evanston · San Francisco · London

Grateful acknowledgment is made for permission to reprint the following:

"Architecture—A Temple of Jehu" by Douglas Haskell from the May 27, 1931, issue of *The Nation*. Reprinted by permission of *Nation*.

"Empire State Building, Part 7: The General Design" by William F. Lamb from *The Architectural Forum*. © 1930 by The Architectural Forum. Reprinted by permission of Architecture Plus, Informat Publishing Corp.

"Everest on 5th Avenue" from the March 25, 1931, issue of *The New York Times*. © 1931 by The New York Times Company. Reprinted by permission.

"Granting the Gold Medal" from the April 23, 1931, issue of *The New York Times*. © 1931 by The New York Times Company. Reprinted by permission.

"The New York That Helen Keller 'Sees'" by Helen Keller, from the January 31, 1932, *New York Times Magazine*. © 1932 by The New York Times Company. Reprinted by permission.

Photograph of King Kong on pages 126–27 reprinted by permission of RKO General, Inc.

FIRST EDITION

Designed by Dorothy Schmiderer

Library of Congress Cataloging in Publication Data

James, Theodore.
  The Empire State Building.
  Bibliography: p.
  Includes index.
  1. New York (City) Empire State Building. I. Title.
F128.8.E46J35 1975   947'.1   74–1821
ISBN 0–06–012172–6

75 76 77 78 79 10 9 8 7 6 5 4 3 2 1

(*Frontispiece*) Aerial view of the Empire State taken in 1954. INP.

Contents

Acknowledgments

I am deeply indebted to my dear friend Elizabeth C. Baker, a long-time enthusiast of the Empire State Building, who suggested that I write this book. Her unflagging loyalty, encouragement, and enthusiasm through the years have been major factors in my career. In addition, I would like to thank Mrs. William F. Lamb, the widow of the architect of the building, and Mrs. Emily Smith Warner, daughter of the late Alfred E. Smith, both of whom shared their reminiscences with me and in so doing gave the book a personal touch. Mr. H. Hamilton Weber, Mr. Daniel Howe and Mr. Robert L. Tinker, all associated with the Empire State Building, are also to be thanked for their cooperation, as is Helmsley-Spear, Inc., without whose interest this book would not have been possible. I would also like to thank Virginia Hilu, my editor at Harper & Row, for her suggestions.

Finally, I would like to thank my mother and father for their assistance with research and typing, and the staffs of the Madison, New Jersey, Public Library and the Avery Library at Columbia University for their kind assistance.

For Betsy Baker with love and thanks

THE EMPIRE STATE LIGHTS

Whence rise you, Lights? *** From this tower built upon Manhattan's native rock. Its roots are deep below forgotten musket balls, the mouldered wooden shoe, the flint, the bone. *** What mark you, Lights? *** Our Nation's doorway. *** Who sleep or toil beneath your good warm gaze? *** All who love this land: they who are of the Land's stout seed, and they who love the Land because they chose to come. *** Sing you a song, Proud Lights? *** We sing silently. We chant a Mass and spiritual, Doxology and Kol Nidre, battle hymn and ballad. We tell of village and of jet—Of wheat and cotton, turbine, oil and goldenrod, the wildest mountains and the cities' roar. *** This is a strange new time. Strong Lights, why never do you fear? *** There is something more powerful. The heart and soul of all Mankind. *** What build you with your beams? A bridge to the stars. *** What offer you to God, O Lights? *** America's devotion.

—MacKinlay Kantor

This tribute appears in bronze just below the Empire State Building's Freedom Lights.

May 3, 1956

1

The Greatest Building in Manhattan

The Empire State Building! The very name immediately brings to mind Manhattan's breathtaking skyline, which it has dominated for close to half a century, in so doing becoming the symbol of the brash vitality and irresistible magnetism of New York, the greatest city in the world. Until recently, it was the tallest building in the world. In 1971, however, in a rather graceless gesture, distinctly lacking in manners and deference, the first of the twin towers of the World Trade Center in Lower Manhattan, designed by architects Minoru Yamasaki and Associates and Emery Roth and Sons, superseded its 102 stories with 8 additional, making it 110 stories or 1,350 feet high. The Empire State Building is no longer the tallest building in Manhattan, but it can still claim to be Manhattan's "greatest" building. Architecturally it is stunning. And in recent years, with the critical reappraisal of the Art Deco style of the 1920s and 1930s, its design has gained even more admiration among cognoscenti.

Ada Louise Huxtable, the distinguished architecture critic for the *New York Times*, recently wrote, in an article entitled "The Skyscraper Style":

1

Don't sell Art Deco short. It is more than high camp or current chic, more than tasseled cigarette cases and streamlined statuettes, more than a passing vogue for one in a series of sentimental stylistic revivals. It has come out of the closet (literally) to be legitimized and dignified, for art history scholars to write about and textbooks to record.

As Style Moderne—the most accepted of a number of sobriquets of which Art Deco is actually a subdivision—it dominated 20th-century art and life for the two decades of the nineteen twenties and thirties. An almost universal design passion or phenomenon at that time, it produced some of the most notable monuments of uniquely American contribution to architectural history, the skyscraper.

Style Moderne is about to take its place in the chronology of serious art movements. But just how, is still the question. Interpretations vary. Some call Style Moderne the dernier cri of the great French decorative arts tradition. Others define it as an initial foray into modernism, as important in its way, as the more generally accepted doctrine of machine art. In its entirety, Style Moderne spanned the period between the two World Wars. It is now a respectable 50-some years old, a time of creaking middle age. Middle age, of course, is when hindsight begins to work.

The Empire State Building's most distinguished characteristic, its shimmering façade, was created by the use of a chrome-nickel-steel alloy plate, which serves both aesthetics and function. The alloy, new at the time, never tarnishes or grows dull. Between each window and its sill, the customary granite or limestone was superseded by a flat plate of dull silver aluminum, sandblasted to obtain a velvety surface. These silver aluminum plates, blending perfectly with the glass of the windows between the sparkling columns of chrome-nickel-steel, make all lines vertical, and impart to the building the appearance of a soaring spire, rising from the base in an uninterrupted sweep to the tower almost one-fifth of a mile above the sky. At sunset, from the New Jersey shoreline of the Hudson River the building is a breathtaking sight as it reflects the fiery orange of the setting sun.

Recently I returned from an extensive trip abroad and took the helicopter from Kennedy Airport across the city. Below, the streetlights ap-

Front view of the Empire State Building,
showing the distinctive chrome-nickel-steel alloy on the façade.
Elizabeth C. Baker.

peared like diamonds gleaming in the night, and the tower of the Empire State hung like a giant chandelier over the incredible creation below. Two young Japanese were on the helicopter, and despite the fact that Yamasaki, a Japanese, had designed the World Trade Center, their excitement at seeing the Empire State was uncontained. I mentioned to them, as we chopped our way across midtown, that the World Trade Center was down there, pointing to the downtown area. They replied, "No, no! The Empire State Building is New York! It is America!" And so it is, and will undoubtedly remain, the symbol of New York, the symbol of America, as the Eiffel Tower is to Paris, Big Ben to London, and Saint Peter's to Rome.

It is still the biggest tourist attraction in the biggest tourist city in the world. On July 15, 1964, during the summer of the World's Fair, for example, 14,575 people paid to go to the top. It lures more people than the United Nations, Radio City, or the Statue of Liberty. On an average day between 5,000 and 6,000 adults pay $1.70 and children from five to eleven pay $0.85 to go to the top. First they go to the eighty-sixth floor observatory, where they can buy souvenirs. On the promenade, fenced in with scimitar-like railings, stationary binoculars that cost a dime to use are available. Having had a look at New York with or without binoculars, from 1,050 feet, a visitor then goes up to a smaller, green-glass-enclosed platform on the 102nd floor, 1,250 feet up.

Under ideal weather conditions a man with normal eyesight can see some fifty miles into five states—Massachusetts, Connecticut, New Jersey, Pennsylvania, and of course New York. Objects twenty-five miles away can be identified. But the real thrill is seeing the city itself, picking out the landmarks in miniature and listening to the low, steady, strong hum of the city, not unlike a beehive.

And what is the visitors' favorite question? "Does it sway?"! In fact, the Empire State has received thousands of letters, and long-distance phone calls from such places as London, Mexico City, and San Francisco, to settle wagers on the subject—usually having to do with the extent of the sway, twenty feet being a popular figure. No, the Empire State Building does not sway, it bends. Swaying implies swinging back and forth. Something that bends goes either back or forth, but not both. Before a wind of 110 miles per hour, the building bends 1.48 inches. The anememeter atop the building was blown away during the wind storm that set that record, so it might have been even a bit stronger. In 1956 aeronautical engineers from the Minneapolis-Honeywell Regulator Company installed a gyroscope on the eighty-fifth floor to take the pulse of the building. Their experiments proved conclusively that the Empire State Building's movement off center was never greater than approximately one-quarter inch at any time, thus the measurable movement was only one-half inch —one-quarter inch from the center. According to engineers, this supports the building's reputation as a true engineering masterpiece. No building ever constructed that is perfectly rigid can compare with the Empire State's maximum stability. If the building were absolutely rigid, vibration effects would be so evident to occupants as to be uncomfortable. Structural engineers explain that the building is supported by an elastic steel skeleton, a device that enables the building to give before high winds and yet minimizes the effect.

Frank Powell, the observation tower manager at the Empire State for many years, recalls many incidents. One day a man came up to him and said, "I'm a trumpet soloist. I'd like to play my trumpet on top of the building. All my life I've wanted to." He presented his card—Samuel J. Coury, Salem Depot, New Hampshire. Powell said, "He seemed like a nice chap, so I told him to go ahead. I even went out and listened. You know what he played? 'I'm Sitting on Top of the World.' Fine tune. When he left, I got to figuring he'd go home and brag about it and have no proof. So I got one of our giant souvenir postcards and wrote on it that this would certify that Mr. Coury had played his trumpet up here at such-and-such an hour, and I put the official building stamp on it and shoved it in the mail to him."

Another time, Powell walked into the restaurant at the eighty-sixth-floor observation terrace and found a man lying flat on his back, eyes wide, breathing normally. The man's friends were at a table, staring glumly at him. "Gorblimey, the building tipped and I lost my balance," explained the man, obviously a visiting Englishman. "I can't help it if the others didn't lose theirs."

Questioning revealed that the man had had a rough Atlantic crossing, but all the while the ship was pitching his friends had told him: "This is nothing compared with what you'll get when you get to the top of the Empire State Building. It sways eighteen feet or more."

The man told Powell the building had tipped just as he hung up his hat. Powell examined the hatrack and found that the bolt holding it upright had come loose. When the hat was hung the rack had swayed forward, and the visitor swayed opposite it right on down to the floor.

Powell has also participated in several scatterings of cremation ashes. The first were those of a man born in Manhattan whose family had moved to an Indiana farm when he was young. His will directed that his ashes be loosed from the building's top. His widow performed the rite, waiting for a day with a brisk wind. Another involved those of a New Jersey woman. The first day she met her future husband, he took her up to the top of the Empire State. They went there several times afterwards, and on one of those occasions he proposed to her. When she was dying, she told him she wanted to be cremated and her ashes scattered from the building top. He wept as he carried out her wish.

Nature plays some odd tricks in that part of the atmosphere which reaches from the eighty-sixth floor at 1,050 feet to the tips of the master TV antenna at 1,472 feet. For instance, sometimes it snows up. The clouds unleashing the snow are less than 1,000 feet high, so the wind currents created by the immense canyons that surround the building literally change the direction of the snow. Sometimes, too, the snow is colored red. Dust particles are picked up as the clouds move in from the west and color the snow.

Back in August 1950, five iron workers who were building the TV antenna atop the building were forced from their perch almost a quarter of a mile up in the air because they were being bombarded by pellets that stung. These pellets, which covered the platform almost an inch deep, were identified by experts as barley. The best guess was that it had been blown all the way from the farmlands of the Great Plains. In addition, insects indigenous to areas over 1,500 miles away have been found on the upper parts of the building. And although there is no explanation as to how they get there, every now and then mice are seen scurrying around on the observatory floors.

The air currents play other tricks. Under certain conditions one can fold down the edges of a conical paper cup, fill it with a specific amount of water, and suspend it and several others outside a window at a certain level of the building. The updraft is such under the right weather conditions that the cups will be held in midair, rotating slowly, disobeying gravity.

The building is also the greatest lightning rod ever built. In stormy weather it is under almost continual bombardment, and has been smashed by as much as 200,000 amperes of electricity nine times in twenty minutes. It takes about 1/6000th of an ampere through the heart to kill a human being, but there is no danger. Quite the opposite. The world's biggest lightning rod is not a rod at all; it's a 60,000-ton steel cage that absorbs the force of the strike, protecting buildings within a mile radius. Safe or not, the Empire State is an awesome spectacle when lightning is playing around the top. Flashes have followed the building's contours from the 1,472-foot tip of the TV antenna to the pavements below. Sometimes, when a hand is stuck out the 102nd-floor window, fire—harmless St. Elmo's fire—will run from the fingers. And sometimes, when conditions are right and the eighty-sixth floor is surrounded by static electricity, if you kiss somebody fire will fly from your lips.

In earlier days the Empire State Building furnished information on fogs coming in from the Atlantic, winds and barometric pressure, and the depth of low-hanging clouds at the 1,250-foot level. Those things are discovered electronically now at airfields, but the Empire State Building still gets icing conditions at 1,000 feet before they are known on the ground.

Every spring and fall, during the great bird migration period, the lights at the top of the tower are extinguished. The Audubon Society asked that this be done because thousands of birds, flying south in the fall and north in the spring, smashed against the building. The lights ruined their orientation and they either flew into the building or straight down into the ground.

In order to better understand the beauty of the architectural design of the Empire State Building, a brief sketch of the history of the skyscraper is helpful. Until around the middle of the nineteenth century, commercial buildings of more than four or five stories in height were very rare. Clients were reluctant to build higher because tenants were rarely willing to climb more than five flights of stairs to carry on their business. However, desirable sites in business districts were expensive, and as business organizations multiplied, became larger, and therefore demanded more space, the logical way to make economical use of those sites was to build upwards. It was not until the 1850s that the invention of the elevator safety device by Elisha Graves Otis provided a safe means of vertical transportation. This sprung a revolution in commercial building that gave birth to the age of the modern skyscraper.

The first safe passenger elevator was installed, in 1857, in the Haughwout store (still standing) at the corner of West Broadway and Broome Street, now a New York City landmark. Thereafter the development of the skyscraper as a unique architectural type was fairly rapid. The first taller-than-average building (180 feet compared to 60 feet) to use the potential of the elevator was the Equitable Life Assurance Society Building in New York City, erected between 1868 and 1870 by Arthur Gilman,

Edward Kendall, and George B. Post. In 1873 Post designed the 230-foot-high Western Union Building, and in the same year Richard Morris Hunt designed the 260-foot-high New York Tribune Building. Both were completed in 1875.

Earlier, Philadelphia architects had expressed interest in solutions to this problem that dealt better with structure. In 1849 William L. Johnston introduced, in the eight-story Jayne Building, a steel-granite construction with columns that rose six stories without interruption, creating an illusion of unusual height.

In Chicago, during the last quarter of the nineteenth century, height and structural design were brought together in a unique manner in Major William LeBaron Jenney's Home Life Insurance Company Building (1885), marking a turning point in the construction of tall buildings. An internal metal frame (part cast iron, part wrought iron) supported the dead weight of the floors and roof and the major load of the ten-story building, eliminating the necessity for immense foundations and thick bearing walls that had previously made structures of this height uneconomical.

Iron had been used in architecture for some time before the mid-nineteenth century, when European and United States architects and engineers exploited its structural advantages in diverse buildings. In 1849, in New York City, James Bogardus erected the Harper Building in which a rigid frame of cast iron columns and beams was the main support for the floor and roof loads. This represented a transition between the old masonry concept and the system used by Jenney in Chicago, in which the interior frame carried not only the roof and floor loads but the weight of the outer walls as well.

During the 1870s, in the American East and Midwest, a reaction developed against the "gingerbread" decorative treatment typical of Victorian architecture. American architects began to design surfaces more or less free of ornament, accenting the basic structure, or "skull and bones," of their buildings.

Then in 1890 a major breakthrough occurred. Late one afternoon

Louis Sullivan strode into the Chicago office of his chief draftsman, Frank Lloyd Wright, and proudly tossed on the table the manila sketch on which he had drawn the elevation of Saint Louis's Wainwright Building. "Look at it," Sullivan commanded. "It's tall!"

And it was tall, every line of it. It was in the design of this building that Louis Sullivan first gave logic and form to the skyscraper, and in so doing heralded the start of modern skyscraper architecture. Sullivan's genius conceived the tall office building as a great unity, infused "with a single germinal idea, which shall permeate the mass and its every detail with the same spirit." As Frank Lloyd Wright later said, "Until Louis Sullivan showed the way, the high buildings lacked unity. They were built up in layers like a great wedding cake. All were fighting height instead of gracefully and honestly accepting it."

At the time, American and European architecture was still in the clutches of Victorian revivalism. In France there was a preference for an ornate and florid neoclassicism, while in the United States high fashion was represented by the more historically correct eclecticism of McKim, Mead and White, a firm adept at applying Renaissance forms to such large structures as Boston's Public Library and the University Club in New York City. Meanwhile, the Art Nouveau movement was taking form as a reaction against the vulgarity of the machine.

The phenomenon of Sullivan's emergence as the first great giver of form to modern architecture must be attributed partially to a very active half century of engineering discovery. James Bogardus's Harper Building, done with prefabricated cast-iron façades and columns, although highly vulnerable to fire, did make iron and glass familiar construction materials for an entire generation of American architects. The inventions of fireproofing and Otis's safe steam elevator, along with Major William LeBaron Jenney's use of the new Bessemer-steel beams and columns, just developed for railroads, in his Home Insurance Building (Chicago, 1885), proving that steel could hold up buildings and walls as well, all were brought together by Sullivan in his skyscraper, the Wainwright Building.

So pressing was the need for office space in business districts that in Chicago architects raised taller and taller buildings. But these had masonry walls, the immense weight of which caused some buildings to sink as much as eighteen inches into the ground. In Burnham and Root's seventeen-story Monadnock Building, the tallest masonry building ever created, the walls were twelve feet thick at the base.

In 1889, a year before the Wainwright Building, Sullivan and his highly talented engineering partner, Dankmar Adler, also tried their hand at masonry construction. Their Auditorium Building in Chicago, with its handsome opera house, was one of the wonders of architecture when it was completed. However, Eiffel's great tower in Paris, finished in the same year, pointed the way. Sullivan, who had long felt that "the engineers were the only men who could face a problem squarely," was quick to capitalize on their discoveries.

To begin to understand why Sullivan's Wainwright Building led the way to the modern skyscraper and therefore to understand the architectural conception of the Empire State Building, we need only turn to his article "The Tall Office Building Artistically Considered," which appeared in *Lippincott's Magazine* in March of 1896. In this article he first articulated his famous dictum "form follows function," one of the earliest major postulates of modern architecture. He said, "It is of the very essence of every problem that it contains and suggests its own solutions."

Thus Sullivan analyzed the function of the different areas in a skyscraper. The ground floor was to contain banks or shops. A second floor was to be a mezzanine, with access provided by a stairway, so this space Sullivan set behind a series of piers. From the third floor to the top were to be an indefinite number of stories of offices, tier upon tier, one identical to the others—for as Sullivan wrote, "Where the function does not change, the form is not to change." On the top he placed a large cornice, ". . . a broad expanse of wall, its dominating weight and character announcing that the series of office tiers had come definitely to an end."

His analysis was lucid, and as is often the case, brilliant in its simplicity, but the architect was not yet finished.

We must now heed the imperative voice of emotion. It demands of us what is the chief characteristic of the tall office building? And at once we answer, it is lofty. This loftiness is to the artistic nature its thrilling aspect. It is the very open organ-tone of its appeal. . . . It must be tall, every inch of it tall. The force and power of altitude must be in it, the glory and pride of exaltation must be in it. It must be every inch a proud and soaring thing, rising in sheer exultation that from bottom to top it is a unity without a single dissenting line.

The partnership of Sullivan and Dankmar Adler was terminated by the panic of 1893. Sullivan continued working for close to ten years after, up in his office in the Auditorium Building, but success slowly eluded him. The last thirty years of his life bred only failure and neglect. Bitterly, he blamed the large eastern architectural establishment, who had turned Chicago's World's Columbian Exposition of 1893 into a showcase for classic-revival architecture. "Architecture, be it known, is dead," he wrote. Later, Frank Lloyd Wright said, "They buried Sullivan and they almost buried me."

Sullivan died in obscurity in 1924, but he left behind him an irrevocable mark on the history of architecture, the skyscraper.

The early decade of this century in New York saw the erection of the landmark Flatiron Building by Daniel H. Burnham in 1902. This building was the first "steel cage" building to approximate the familiar modern type of architecture, although the exterior design is that not of a steel but of a stone building. A few years later Cass Gilbert designed the Gothic-inspired Woolworth Building, but it was not until the late 1920s and early 1930s, with the erection of the Chrysler Building and the Empire State Building, that Louis Sullivan's concept that "form follows function" was again expressed in skyscraper architecture.

2

The Most Valuable Property in the World

Almost one hundred and seventy-five years ago, the site of the Empire State Building at Fifth Avenue and Thirty-fourth Street was a small meadow located on one of the most charming farms of Manhattan Island. In the spring, dogtooth violets, spring beauties, trillium, and jack-in-the-pulpits greeted the returning hordes of bluebirds, goldfinches, and vireos, while in the summer daisies, wild strawberries, blackberries, and raspberries were there for the picking. A bubbling brook filled with trout and "sunnies" gently crossed the property. Brant goose, black duck, and yellowleg splashed in the waters, and fox, rabbit, and partridge found cover in the surrounding thickets.

The only apparent sign of civilization was an occasional wagon trundling up or down a dirt lane called Bloomingdale Road, which lay just slightly to the west, the original trail of today's Broadway, the city's first main thoroughfare of any considerable length, or perhaps a horse and rider on the old Middle Road, just to the east, over in the direction of today's bustling Madison Avenue.

At the turn of the century—the eighteenth, that is—Fifth Avenue was not even on the map. Today's Washington Square Park at the foot of Fifth Avenue, Madison Square Park at Twenty-third Street, and today's Bryant Park behind the Public Library were potter's fields, where the poor and unknown were buried in anonymous graves, and places of execution, where the gallows performed their grisly duties.

New York as such lay far to the south, in what is today the financial district of Lower Manhattan. The residential areas of the more-or-less middle-class merchants of English and Dutch extraction were on Stuyvesant Square, Lafayette Street, and the presently nonexistent Saint John's Square. Lower Second Avenue had its share of substantial houses, while Wall Street and Battery Park were promenades for the local gentry.

The southern boundary of today's Greenwich Village was still largely fields and pastureland. Where Greenwich Street ended at the Hudson River, fishermen were seen at the end of the day, pulling in their nets full of fish. The streets that did exist were narrow and crooked, and the Bowery was still a dusty country lane lined with tiny cottages and farms. The Boston Post Road meandered north to what is now Madison Square, where it turned and continued on through Harlem and eventually reached Boston.

Had you wandered down a typical street of the period, you would have seen rows of Dutch-shuttered brick houses, whose characteristic stoops, leading to the front doors, still predominate on most of the residential streets of New York today. Inside the ladies of the houses entertained their friends at tea in the afternoon and at elaborate and very long dinners in the evening. One or two servants, usually black or recently arrived Irish women, assisted with the housework. Candles lighted the tables at dinner; oil lamps, the rest of the house.

On a typical weekday morning, the streets teemed with activity. Dressed in cotton frocks and cloaks, the mistresses of the houses shopped at markets or peddlers' wagons for the food for the day. Wild boar, wild turkey, wild duck, wild geese, venison, partridge, and squab filled the markets. Fresh fruits and vegetables were available in season only, and the tomato, or love apple, was not found anywhere, as it was still believed to be poisonous. Chimneys sweeps, milkmen, fishmongers, and peddlers all filled the air with cries of their wares, and hot corn girls walked barefoot in the streets shouting. "Hot corn! Hot corn! Here's your lily-white hot corn!" Others sold fresh mint, wild strawberries and blackberries, radishes, and hot yams. The area north of Canal Street was rural—in short, "the sticks," with much of it common land.

In that year of 1799, John Thomson contracted, and paid $2,600, for the land for his farm site, upon which the majestic, glimmering grandeur of the architectural triumph that has become the worldwide symbol of New York City, if not of America itself, now stands—the Empire State Building.

When Thomson bought the land, it was still an untilled tract of virgin land. Old city records describe it as "that certain piece of land formerly parcel of the commonlands of the Mayor, Aldermen and Commonalty of the City of New York . . . released and conveyed to John Thomson by Indenture dated the sixteenth day of March A.D. 1799."

The farm comprised an area of the six present blocks now bounded by Broadway and Sixth Avenue on the west, Madison Avenue on the east, and Thirty-third and Thirty-sixth streets on the south and north. It stretched across the present city plan on a bias, and was intersected by Sunfish Creek, which originated from a spring on current Fifty-seventh Street just west of Broadway and poured into Sunfish Pond at the foot of present Park Avenue. It was one of the dozens of brooks that once crisscrossed the island but are now either totally lost or flowing through pipes far below the streets of the city, every now and then wreaking havoc with New York's compulsive "progress" by reemerging in the most peculiar places and at the most inopportune times.

The brook approached the present Empire State Building property along Thirty-fourth Street, near the present northern entrance to the building. In the middle of the skyscraper's site it was joined by another short brook, which was fed by a stream. The joining of the two brooks formed a natural fishing hole, and according to letters and diaries that still exist today, "many a fine mess of sunfish and eels were hooked" where visitors today board the express elevators to the tower.

Even though prior to 1799 these were nondescript "commonlands," the Thomson farm had played an important part in the American Revolution some twenty-odd years before. Many a musket ball had landed in its soil, if musket balls could indeed carry a distance of two blocks, for an important battle between the colonists and the British once took place within the long shadow now cast by the skyscraper on the surrounding area. Albert Ullian, the historian, points out that "America came so near to losing the Revolution within the Thirty-fourth Street area that it is anything but uncomfortable for a patriot to contemplate!" The battle occurred when the British succeeded in landing their army at Kips Bay Farm, presently the site of the Kips Bay apartment complex, at the foot of Thirty-fourth Street near the East River, on September 15, 1776, after the disastrous Battle of Long Island.

On that day stray shots began to fall on what is now Fifth Avenue in what has come to be called the "battle of the cornfield," fought near Kips Bay. Apparently, General George Washington himself had rushed down from his headquarters in the Jumel Mansion, which still stands on 160th Street, and taken up his position on a small knoll at Fifth Avenue and Forty-second Street, where the Public Library now stands.

The colonial army was in rout, running straight for him. It appeared as though the redcoats would break through the colonial defenses, cross Sunfish Creek, cut Manhattan in half, and succeed in trapping 3,500 American troops still down in Lower Manhattan.

According to the letter of Colonel Tench Tilghman, the general's aide-de-camp, Washington "laid his cane over many of the officers who shewed their men the example of running!!"

In the nick of time, General Israel Putnam arrived with reinforcements, and a rally was effected as he was sent downtown along Sunfish Creek and Bloomingdale Road to rescue and direct the 3,500 men out of Lower Manhattan.

That battle was fought on the famous Murray Farm, from which the Murray Hill section of today's New York derives its name. It was here that the overconfident redcoats paused complacently for their midday meal on the grass on the trim grounds of the Murray house, named "Incleberg," which stood at what is now Thirty-seventh Street and Madison Avenue. Officers Howe, Clinton, and Cornwallis and New York Governor Tryon were all there. A legend persists that Mrs. Murray, the mother of Lindley Murray, the grammarian, "saved the army." An acquaintance of Tryon, who apparently introduced her to the British generals that afternoon, she invited them into her elegant parlors, tempted them bountifully with wine and cakes, flirted with General Howe enticingly, and loitered in light and frivolous conversation for two hours. It was, or so the story goes, a desperate attempt to save General Putnam and his men marching south past the farm just to the west, on or near the present site of the Empire State Building.

Donald Barr Chidsey, the historian, in *The Tide Turns*, reflects doubt that Mrs. Murray was "a sort of colonial Cleopatra." He claims she could hardly have known that General Putnam, or "Old Put," as he was referred to, was on his way to Lower Manhattan. He himself didn't know until the last minute, when General Washington sent him south, that that was where he was headed. In addition, Mrs. Murray was Quaker, disapproving of war, and a Tory, disapproving of rebellion. As Chidsey says, "Moreover, she was in her fifties and the mother of twelve children, hardly one to turn seductress at a moment's notice." At any rate, whether or not Mrs. Murray was responsible, the men were saved.

John Thomson's farm lay just a stone's throw from the historic farm of Robert Murray, separated from it by the Middle Road, which ran diagonally from Madison Avenue and Thirty-fourth Street to Fifth Avenue and Forty-second Street. No records exist as to where Thomson's house stood, but it undoubtedly occupied part of the Empire State site, in order to be near Sunfish Brook and the spring.

Fresh water was not only valuable in those days, but scarce as well. The only other available water source in the vicinity of the site was a duck pond that lay two blocks west of Henry Meigs' six-acre farm, near the present corner of Seventh Avenue and Thirty-fourth Street. A picture of the pond, drawn by Henry Meigs' son, "who shot a muscrat [sic] in it," is in the archives at the New-York Historical Society. And when Meigs entertained the French consul to New York, the Conte d'Espinville, at dinner during his tenure in this country, he served delectable frogs' legs from the bullfrogs who croaked away in that pond.

There seems to be no record of the sale of Thomson's farm; however, an advertisement proclaiming the sale has survived. It reads:

F O R   S A L E
TO BE SOLD,

A new and convenient house, barn and several out-houses, together with twenty acres of land, very pleasantly situated in the heart of New York Island, along the Middle Road, near the 3 mile stone, about ½ mile North from Chelsea Village. The land is fertile, partly wooded and well watered, and eminently suitable for the raising of various produce, profitably disposed of to the opulent families of the City. It is confidently expected by those whose opinions are conceded to be found, that the rapid growth of the City and of the Villages of Greenwich and Chelsea will soon cause the value of the Aforesaid Land to be greatly enhanced.

The subscriber's only motive for disposing of the above place is that circumstances require his removal to the City. For further particulars, enquire of the subscriber on the premises.

JNO. THOMSON.

Apparently, the handbill resulted in the sale, because a deed was recorded "at the request of W. C. Wetmore the 24th day of September 1825 at fifty minutes past 3:00 P.M." that states that "one Thomas and Margaret, his wife," sold the same farm to Charles Lawton for $10,000. At that time, there wasn't so much as a surveyor's stake to mark what is now Fifth Avenue and Thirty-fourth Street. If anyone had told those simple farm owners in 1825 that they were crazy to sell out for only $10,000, they probably would have replied guilelessly, "This place only cost twenty-six hundred dollars twenty-six years ago."

Two years later, on July 28, 1827, the Lawtons garnered double their investment when they sold the farm to William Backhouse Astor, the second son of "robber baron" John Jacob Astor. He, like his father before him and his sons after him, firmly believed in investing in New York City real estate, which, incidentally, included among other things opium dens, brothels, and later barely habitable tenement housing. However, it was to be many years before actual streets were cut through the property.

Nine years later, in 1836, Thirty-fourth Street was staked out right through to the Hudson River. Near the river in that year, close to the present corner of Ninth Avenue, a corner stone was being laid for the new New York Institute for the Blind. The locale was then a remote, bucolic part of town near the old Glass House Farm, which stood overlooking the Hudson and the green shores of New Jersey. That end of Thirty-fourth Street was known as Hudson Place.

Meanwhile, Astor patiently awaited the northward advance of the city. He faithfully believed in the future of the area, although he still lived on what is today Lafayette Street, across from the present home of Joseph Papp's New York Free Public Theater, the former Astor Library, in a house that, amazingly enough, still stands today as the faded shadow of a once splendidly elegant residential area, Colonnade Row.

In 1830 the city had taken title to the Fifth Avenue road rights as far north as Twenty-fourth Street. And then, in 1834, Henry C. Brevoort built his "country mansion" at the northwest corner of Fifth Avenue and Ninth Street, a building that stood as recently as 1925. Their move was a bold one that proved to be a clever one. Apparently Astor, who had yet to attain any social recognition among New York's elite of the period, kept a keen eye on their move. Since the Brevoorts were socially prominent, their decision to build on Fifth Avenue caused nothing short of a run on the real estate they owned all the way to Twentieth Street. One by one the lots were sold and the social sheep ensconced themselves as Brevoort neighbors. Astor became even more firmly convinced that one day his investment would pay off. In 1837–38, the city took title to Fifth Avenue as far north as 129th Street.

In 1842, when Charles Dickens paid his first visit to the city, he visited some of the elegant town houses that had been built on lower Fifth Avenue, and the following year James Lenox, whose superb collection of rare books and manuscripts eventually became part of the nucleus of the New York Public Library collection, moved into his mansion on the northeast corner of Twelfth Street and Fifth Avenue.

Elegant churches were built during the 1840s, including the Church of the Ascension, the scene of President John Tyler's wedding to "fleshy" Julia Gardiner of the Gardiner's Island Gardiners, at Tenth Street and Fifth Avenue. Within a few years the First Presbyterian Church was built between Eleventh and Twelfth; the South Dutch Reformed Church, on the southeast corner of Twenty-first Street; the Fifth Avenue Presbyterian Church, at Nineteenth Street, and the Marble Collegiate, way up on Twenty-ninth Street in 1854.

By the 1850s Fifth Avenue as far north as Twenty-third Street was solidly lined with elegant town houses, churches, and clubs, and in 1854 the Brevoort Hotel, which remained the last word in elegance for almost a century, was opened. Astor watched as John Taylor Johnston, Lispenard Stewart, Isaac M. Singer, and General David Sickles all took up residence on the Avenue. It was during this era that "The Fifth Avenue" began to be mentioned in guidebooks and foreign diaries, always in the most glowing terms. In 1853 *The Stranger's Handbook for the City of New York; or What to See and How to See It* described the avenue as "the most magnificent street on this continent if not yet the finest in the world. The imposing dwellings of the city's leading residents have caused Fifth Avenue to supersede Broadway in the interest of the visiting public."

A year or so later, Lord Acton, in his *American Diaries*, confirmed the fact that Fifth Avenue had become the most elegant street in the city. "The 'great people' of the city no longer live on Broadway but on Fifth

Avenue. Here impressive structures of brown sandstone, or a richly decorated style of architecture, lend quietude and splendor to this New World Belgravia."

Then in 1850, August Belmont, a German-Jewish immigrant who had attained social acceptance and later social supremacy in the city by marrying Caroline Slidell Perry, daughter of Commodore Matthew Perry, moved into his elaborate mansion on the northwest corner of Eighteenth Street. With the opening of the Belmont house, Fifth Avenue entered a new phase of its history. Now it was no longer strictly the home of the original Hudson Valley Dutch- and English-descended families. It became the symbol for socially aspiring new money.

Old Commodore Vanderbilt had no interest in social climbing, being content to live a quiet life, and the Astors remained on Lafayette Place in Colonnade Row. Their property up on Fifth Avenue at Thirty-fourth Street was still virtually an outlying country road. In fact, the city directory of that year enumerated the houses only as far north as Twenty-third Street, and then stopped. "Beyond Twenty-third Street, in 1850," states *Valentine's Manual* by Henry Collins Brown, "the Avenue, while cut through, was as yet unpaved and the sides fell off perceptibly from the street level." In many areas just to the north of Twenty-third Street, farmers and squatters lived. On December 9, 1851, the *New York Times* reported:

A few days ago a man by the name of Cornelius Sullivan was arrested by the 19th Ward police, charged with violating the law by persisting in skinning dead horses in 40th and 42nd Streets, just off Fifth Avenue, to the great annoyance of residents in that section of the city. He was sentenced to six months in prison as a caution to men who are in the habit of skinning dead horses or other animals in that area.

But William Astor realized that it would be a matter of only a decade or so before his land at Thirty-fourth Street would be worth a small fortune.

Interestingly enough, the first efforts at "skyscraping" were made during this period, within a few blocks of the Empire State Building site. Flimsy wooden buildings had sprung up like mushrooms in the area of the present Madison Square Garden complex at Seventh Avenue and Thirty-third Street. A fire tower designed by architect James Bogardus rose 100 feet on iron columns. It looked much like the Bogardus Tower, still standing in Mount Morris Park, on Fifth Avenue in Harlem. A circular iron stairway led up to a large bell, from which New Yorkers, in the year of 1851, saw a view as sensational to them then as the view from the Empire State Building tower is to us today.

Plans for the first World's Fair to be held in New York City were attracting attention out in the squatter's section near the New York City Reservoir, which had been built on the site of the present New York City Public Library. The city's first real skyscraper, the timber-framed Latting Observatory, was built in 1853 on the north side of Forty-second Street, just west of Fifth Avenue, coinciding with the opening of the Fair. It rose to the dizzy height of 350 feet, about one-quarter the height of the Empire State Building, but it failed financially because very few people dared to go up in its steam elevator. It offered the city one of the greatest spectacles in its history when it went up in flames in 1856.

In 1859 the first of the Astors finally decided it was time to move from Colonnade Row to the site of the Empire State Building. The newspapers informed their readers that a "mansion presenting a rather unique appearance has been erected by John Jacob Astor, Jr., on the Fifth Avenue at the corner of Thirty-third Street. It is faced with Philadelphia pressed brick, and the window dressings, architraves, cornices, rustic columns and stoop are made of Nova Scotia freestone." J. J. Astor had married Charlotte Gibbs of Philadelphia, a cultivated, gracious, well-traveled, benign philanthropist, who possessed the most extraordinary diamonds in the United States. This was the first of the "twin Astor houses."

Several years later, J. J.'s brother, William Backhouse, built his house just north of his brother's on the southwest corner of Fifth Avenue and

Thirty-fourth Street. William B. had married Caroline Schermerhorn, who eventually became known as "the" Mrs. Astor. "The" Mrs. Astor unfortunately lacked both beauty and brains, and in fact, wore a black wig because she was bald. She was, however, worth $50 million, and had an "old" New York family background and the personality and determination of a Prussian drill sergeant. The William Astors' four-story brownstone mansion, which became "the" center of New York's social life for many years, was built at a cost of $1,500,000 and a further cost of $750,000 to furnish. In the ballroom at the rear of Mrs. Astor's house and that of her in-laws, which they shared, the supreme event of New York's social season was held. Every year, on the third Monday of January, she gave a ball, limiting her guest list to four hundred people. The term "the Four Hundred" derives from her list. Ward McAllister, her social arbiter, an ignominious fop and hanger-on, once told a reporter, "There are only about four hundred people in fashionable New York society, don't you know. If you go outside the number, don't you see, you strike people who are either not at ease in a ballroom or else make other people not at ease. See the point?"

At her annual gala, Mrs. Astor received while standing in front of a full-length oil portrait of herself. Her jewels, including an immense diamond stomacher said to have belonged to Marie Antoinette, were worn in excessive and vulgar display. After her death, it was learned that her famous rope of pearls was partly fake; only every other pearl was genuine.

Today, as you stand near the rear of the Empire State Building's main lobby, you will be near the spot where "the" Mrs. Astor received her guests. It is interesting to note that many of the names on her list of "Four Hundred" are seldom, if ever, heard of today. Theodore Roosevelt, an assortment of Livingstons, Hamiltons, Schermerhorns, Remsens, and de Rhams were all invited, among many others whose families have since faded into oblivion.

The twin Astor houses were the indirect result of the erection opposite

(Overleaf) Site of the Empire State Building, Fifth Avenue and 34th Street as it looked in 1895. The first of the Astor houses is on the right.

Madison Square of the historic Fifth Avenue Hotel, which, as the Waldorf-Astoria was destined to do later, gave New York's social center a jolt that sent the residential district pioneering northward. At the same time the Astor houses, with their Nova Scotia freestone, sandstone, or brownstone, spurred the city's building spree that plastered the town with brownstone fronts.

When the first Astor house was built, the Broadway Tabernacle, long located on Worth Street, on the east side of lower Broadway, moved uptown, a block to the west of the Empire State site. Christ Church established itself just a block north of the Astor homes, on part of the site of the present B. Altman & Company department store. The quiet residential character of the neighborhood was further attended when the Fourth Presbyterian Church was built on Thirty-fourth Street, across from the present Macy's Department Store. This took place in 1867, the year Dr. Sarsaparilla Townsend's house was torn down by A. T. Stewart, the merchant prince, and his so-called Marble Palace was erected facing William B. Astor's house from the northwest corner of Fifth Avenue and Thirty-fourth Street.

Ten years later, during the post-Civil War "flash era" of the 1870s, the prestige of the district reached its peak with the establishment of the University Club just to the north. The New York Club took over the corner at the dawn of the 1880s to enjoy that elegant decade there, but the approach of the business invasion, and the growth of the nearby "tenderloin" on Broadway and Sixth Avenue, were destined to disturb the peace.

The "tenderloin," a goal of every ambitious police captain, acquired its sobriquet when Inspector Alexander (Clubber) Williams took it over and declared that he had eaten chuck steak long enough and now would enjoy some tenderloin. It was the haunt of the old-time actor, pugilist, and turfman, and as the theaters pushed up Sixth Avenue, Thirty-fourth Street, with its junction of horse-car lines, became the focus of the show world. It was no longer necessary for a flagman to stand under the elevated railway structure to warn equestrians from nearby town houses of the approach of the puffing, steam-propelled elevated trains. In that section, New York was becoming hardened.

Here the bedizened of Sixth Avenue mingled with their less garish sisters of the then elegant Broadway. Here were grouped a number of famous bars and restaurants. Gentleman Jim Corbett, the boxer who trounced John L. Sullivan, was the proprietor of the former Parker's, a popular bar on Broadway near where the central door of Korvettes Department Store swings now. George Boldt, who later became a partner in the Waldorf-Astoria, had been a waiter in Parker's. It was a sort of poor man's Delmonico's then, but had fallen into the hands of one Charley White and a declining clientele when Corbett came along.

Seventh Avenue in the vicinity of the present Madison Square Garden had developed into a string of old clothes dealers, cobblers' shops, and squalid barracks that temporarily filled the gap for blacks before the jump to Harlem. Such was the trend of growth in the area during the post-Civil War period.

In 1887 John Jacob Astor, Jr., died, and his wife, the lovely Charlotte, withdrew, leaving Caroline Astor to rule the roost. Charlotte's son, William Waldorf Astor, then inherited the southern of the two twin houses. William, or "Willie" as he was called, was ambitious for his wife, neé Mary Paul of Philadelphia, and resented deeply his aunt's domination of society. After having run for Congress twice in his district and losing both times, he decided to move to London, eventually becoming Baron Astor of Cliveden, thus the English branch of the Astor family. It was into this branch that Nancy Langhorne of Virginia married, to become the famed Lady Astor, recently deceased. Whether it was done to spite his imperious aunt, who lived next door, or the district that had snubbed him at the polls, or whether it was a simple matter of good business, "Willie" decided to build the Waldorf, his memorial to America. He intended to give New York a hotel befitting the city. His great structure

The old Waldorf-Astoria, which stood at Fifth Avenue
and 34th Street until 1929, when it was demolished
to make way for the Empire State Building.

was to be built on the southern half of the Fifth Avenue block front, an elaborate, red brick and sandstone German Renaissance edifice that was to startle the country. Among its features were to be murals and elegantly appointed salons copped from palaces of the Second Empire.

Upon hearing of the plans, the denizens of Fifth Avenue fell into a snit. "Think of the neighborhood," they said. "It's the end of Fifth Avenue. First the trolleys and now this!" There was talk of a monumental snub. There was talk of legal action. After all, Fifth Avenue was a place to live. One didn't work on Fifth Avenue or entertain outside the confines of one's mansion, except for occasional dinners at Delmonico's or at the "traditional" Brevoort and the Fifth Avenue Hotel at Madison Square. This new hotel would invariably attract only travelers from the Middle West and "bad elements." Nevertheless, Astor, who had already finalized his plans to get out of town, razed his house and went ahead with erecting the thirteen-story Waldorf Hotel on the corner of Fifth Avenue and Thirty-third Street. He hired Henry J. Hardenbergh, a fashionable architect at the time, to design the hotel and signed George Boldt, who had since become proprietor of the Bellevue in Philadelphia, as manager. In November of 1890 he filed the plans with the New York City Building Department. Wrecking crews started gnawing away at the Astor house, and presently cabbies would detour in front of the gaping hole to crane their necks at the workmen erecting the foundation piers. Two years later, on Monday, March 13, 1893, the building opened.

On opening night, "Willie" Astor's wife decided to throw a benefit concert in the hotel for Saint Mary's Free Hospital for Children, her favorite charity. She hired Walter Damrosch and all the boys from the New York Symphony Orchestra for the evening. Now, Damrosch could be counted on as a good draw. The charity was impeccable. The sumptuous new hotel was a curiosity. Throw in Mrs. Astor and the waxworks assembled. From Chicago came, not the butchers, but Mrs. Potter Palmer and Mr. and Mrs. George Pullman, in one of their private Pullmans. From Boston came Lawrences, Amorys, Lowells, Dexters and Peabodys. From Philadelphia, Biddles, Lippincotts, Cadwaladers and Drexels. And of course, from New York, Fishes, Hamiltons, Havemeyers, Jays, Lorillards, Morrises, Dodges, and all those people.

The ushers at the concert were men selected to "represent the flower of the Union, Knickerbocker and Calumet Clubs," to quote the *New York Times* of the day. To sum up, there was no ballroom fodder at this affair. It was strictly glitter and glow, from start to finish. The Waldorf was established as "in" with the jet set of its day.

Fifteen hundred super society celebrities traipsed through a downpour to view the new hotel. One by one the guests disembarked from their carriages and swept into the great, palm-bedecked drawing room, where the ladies of the committee received in their second-best gowns—for the rain had regaled a spirit of sense instead of splash. They inspected the edifice —the $5 million hotel with its 450 rooms, 350 of them with baths—from stem to stern. They saw the eight private dining rooms, all arranged to serve the *côtelettes de ris de veau*, oysters, terrapin, *glace a l'orange*, and *glace fantaisie*. One of these was an exact reproduction of the dining room of the old Astor mansion that had formerly stood on the spot, and in which much of the old Astor furniture and service were used. And the famed Empire Room was done in the style of the grand salon in Mad King Ludwig's palace in Munich.

Since the opening occurred during Lent, no dancing was permitted; however, this hardly kept the Four Hundred times four away. Many of those who arrived late found no seats available for the concert. The opening was covered elaborately in the press, the *New York Sun* writing:

Louis XIV could not have got the likes of the first suite of apartments set apart for the most distinguished guests of the hotel. There is a canopied bed upon a dais, such as a king's should be. Upon this couch shall repose the greatnesses, and, looking about them, see many thousands of dollars' worth of fineries. Think of the joy of being great!

The *New York Times* added:

The opening of a large hotel by society, is a frequent occurrence in England and on the Continent, where the handsomest and most renowned establishments in the various European capitals have been opened by royalty itself with festivities of a brilliant character. It is novel in this country.

To ascertain the extent of the impact of the Hotel Waldorf on the manners and mores of the era, an anonymous society woman commented on the entire proceedings:

Few homes have chefs. I gave a small affair of eighteen covers at Mi Carême; the game was spoiled, undeniably spoiled and the strawberries were so hard and green it was like biting chestnuts to try to eat them. Such of us, by the way who do not keep these treasures (private chefs) permanently in our service are welcoming the Waldorf with its famous Philadelphia caterer [George Boldt]. It will be one additional high-class place, and will thus relieve the pressure on the two or three other places where all society wants to get service and it will besides stimulate these places to better work through a feeling of rivalry.

And so the Hotel Waldorf opened and changed the ways of the American society that had initially snubbed the entire project.

In addition, "Willie's" wife announced that ladies would be welcome at all times, and publicly secured this image for the hotel by making conspicuous entrances alone at various times of the day and night. The respectability of the hotel was then unquestioned.

During the first month of its operation, the Waldorf, named after the little town of Waldorf, Duchy of Baden, in Germany, the ancestral home of the Astor family, entertained the first of a long group of highly distinguished visitors. A party of Spanish grandees, led by the Duke and Duchess of Veragua, made the Waldorf their home before moving on to attend the famed Chicago World's Fair. The Infanta Eulalia followed, and a reception for her was attended by most of the socially prominent women of New York, Boston, Philadelphia, Washington, Baltimore, and Chicago.

However, all of this was a mere harbinger of what was to come. On February 10, 1897, Mr. and Mrs. Bradley-Martin threw their famous party in the Waldorf that was to mark the end of extravagant galas in the city. The Bradley-Martins came from Troy, New York, but rarely, if ever, mentioned it. Martin, before the hyphen was added to his name, was the son of an attorney whose fortune had been made in the stock market. His wife, Cornelia, believed in Society. They had gone abroad, bought a house in London and a country place in Inverness, and married their daughter off to Lord Craven. Fifth Avenue and New York was the last challenge, and with the encouragement of Ward McAllister and Mrs. Paran Stevens, a contemporary social wheeler and dealer, the couple set out to establish themselves. One morning after reading of the conditions in the slums of the city, Mrs. Martin decided to "give trade an impetus" by staging a costume ball. She ended by spending $369,200.

The Waldorf was selected for the party. The hotel was turned into a replica of the Hall of Mirrors at Versailles, with furniture in the Louis XIV style. Every flower in the city, as well as most of the blossoms available from Baltimore to Boston, was purchased to decorate the ballroom, and hundreds of blooms of clematis, shipped from Alabama, embellished the sylvan dells and flirtation nooks.

Mrs. Martin appeared costumed as Mary, Queen of Scots, and her husband as Louis XV. August Belmont donned a full suit of steel armor inlaid with gold, which cost $10,000. Family jewels were borrowed from impoverished Southern aristocrats; the Oglethorpe gems arrived from Georgia and the Fairfax diamonds from Virginia. Mrs. Martin displayed a massive ruby necklace once worn by Marie Antoinette.

Reports of the party both here and abroad were critical. The *London Chronicle* wrote: "We congratulate New York Society on its triumph. It has cut out Belshazzar's feast and Wardour Street and Mme. Tussaud's and the Bank of England. There is no doubt about that." Oscar Hammerstein produced a burlesque of the fete called *The Bradley-Radley Ball.* Soon the pulpit joined the press in attacking the Martins' extravagance, and the city authorities entered the fray as well, doubling the tax assessments of the Martins' property. The notoriety caused the Martins to move permanently to England.

In the meantime, "the" Mrs. Astor, who was most definitely not on the most friendly terms with her nephew, the hotel builder, sat and stewed. After the Waldorf had thrown its prophetic shadow on her town house, she felt that the neighborhood was going to the dogs, and said as much. "There is," in her words, "a glorified tavern next door." What was more, the A. T. Stewart house across Thirty-fourth Street had been leased to the Manhattan Club for this "mauve decade," and neither she nor her husband relished the sight of "politicians" watching their home from the club windows.

Nonetheless, the Waldorf was a tremendous success both financially and socially, finally convincing the owners of the remaining of the twin houses to sell out and join in the venture. "The" Mrs. Astor's house came down, and she moved into her new house, designed by Richard Morris Hunt, on the southeast corner of Sixty-fifth Street and Fifth Avenue, now the site of Temple Emmanu-El. Richard J. Hardenburgh, the architect of the Waldorf, was hired to design the Astoria, named after Astoria, Oregon, founded in 1811 by John Jacob Astor I at the mouth of the Columbia River. The sensation of its twin was repeated when it opened November 1, 1897. The Waldorf-Astoria was completed, but Mrs. Astor stipulated that, should she change her mind, the two buildings could be separated. On every floor where doorways were constructed to combine the two buildings, provisions were made for sealing them up again.

Shortly after the opening of the Astoria, the Waldorf inaugurated the Monday morning musicales, a fad that remained a society must until World War II. When Ping-Pong became the fad, Ping-Pong tables were installed for the ladies. A free billiard table for patrons was another novelty inaugurated at the Waldorf-Astoria.

Aside from being in the forefront in the matter of novelties, the Waldorf, and particularly manager George Boldt, was a leader in matters of perhaps more permanent importance. He inaugurated room telephones, pneumatic tubes for mail delivery to the upper floors, floor pantries for room service, and floor clerks, all of which have become standard in luxury hotels since.

During its heydey, the old Waldorf hosted an impressive array of royal and noted visitors. The crown prince of Siam, who later as king was one of the first dignitaries to visit the observation tower of the Empire State Building, and Prince Henry of Prussia both stayed at the Waldorf in its early days. Edward, then Prince of Wales; the sister and brother-in-law of the emperor of Japan; Li Hung-chang, the viceroy of China; Viscount Kitchener of Khartoum; Guglielmo Marconi; and every American President who held office during its existence, all were guests at the old Waldorf. The plans for the Panama Canal were first made in a room in the hotel, and the United States Steel Corporation was formed in another.

When the king and queen of the Belgians arrived after World War I, painters worked day and night redecorating an entire floor of the hotel. The royal entourage consisted of 40 people—maids, secretaries, ladies-in-waiting—and the royal couple's 160 pieces of luggage. Private telephones were installed, and six cooks were assigned to prepare meals for the party.

At the time of the *Titanic* disaster, the Waldorf threw open its doors to survivors who arrived in New York on the *Carpathia*. It became the clearing house for news of survivors and for tearful reunions with loved ones.

Admiral Dewey and King Carol of Rumania (traveling incognito when he was prince), Prince Poniatowsky, Lord and Lady Decies, Cardinal Mercier, Lloyd George, Marshal Foch, and Ambassador Jusserand, all stayed at the Waldorf. Buffalo Bill, Lillian Russell, Diamond Jim Brady, and John L. Sullivan were regular denizens of its public rooms. The list is endless. The Waldorf had become New York's unofficial palace; and its location, the heart of the city's social life.

Its famous "Peacock Alley," its social triumphs and the Astoria restaurant at the Thirty-fourth Street corner "marked the partial eclipse of

Delmonico's" in the estimation of more than one commentator. The latter establishment was still holding forth at Twenty-sixth Street, where it had moved in the uptown trek from the Union Square district. Soon it and all others who would cater to the elite were to move uptown before the wedge of the Waldorf-Astoria.

Just as the Fifth Avenue Hotel had blazed the way at Madison Square fifty years before, the Waldorf was now the leader. It was a long time since the old Astor House in Lower Broadway, just north of Saint Paul's Chapel, had held the apex of the social ladder.

With the Waldorf-Astoria came business. McCreery's moved up from the Twenty-third Street shopping district, as did Best and Company and Bonwit Teller. B. Altman and Company made their move to midtown in 1906, locating first at Sixth Avenue and Twenty-first Street, then at Sixth Avenue at Nineteenth Street, finally moving to the northeast corner of Fifth Avenue and Thirty-fourth Street, where they remain to this day, diagonally across from the Empire State Building. While they were building, the town was full of rumors that Marshall Field of Chicago was coming in. Macy's, which had been at Sixth Avenue and Fourteenth Street since 1858, moved to Herald Square in 1902. Tiffany's, too, held forth long in the Union Square neighborhood, and then moved north to the midtown area.

The building of Pennsylvania Station at Seventh Avenue and Thirty-fourth Street was a tremendous factor in the development of that district. The terminal, one of the largest buildings in the world, ranked close in size to the Vatican and Tuilleries and required six years to build; it stood until recently on the site of the present Madison Square Garden complex. Penn Station brought many changes with it. The new Post Office followed; it was constructed on Eighth Avenue, where it still stands. The Pennsylvania Hotel, now the Statler, was erected, and then the Governor Clinton and the Hotel New Yorker.

With the retail business definitely established in the midtown area, aside from the notable exceptions of Wanamakers and Hearn's, other businesses followed. The fur center eventually moved up from Canal Street to establish its five thousand firms to the south of Pennsylvania Station. The extensive garment center then moved into the section north of the station, into the deep Seventh Avenue canyon of today. Millinery was another one of the early invaders of this district. Then the textile industry moved over from lower Madison and Fifth avenues, attracted by the large new buildings being built between Herald and Times squares.

Throughout the Roaring Twenties, the Waldorf-Astoria continued to be New York's social center. However, real estate values in the midtown area were climbing dramatically. All up and down Fifth Avenue, the dust of demolition was in the air, as the great building boom of the mid-twenties ended the golden age of Fifth Avenue. Apartment houses, office buildings, and department stores replaced the elaborate mansions, clubs, churches, and restaurants of the area.

Early in 1925 boulevardiers looked on in horror at the corner of Forty-fourth Street and Fifth Avenue as the walls of the famous Red Room of Delmonico's came barreling down the chutes into a waiting dump cart, and gas torches began to slice through the steel structure around them. Two years before, the famed Sherry's had met a similar fate. Prohibition, coupled with soaring real estate values in the area, had doomed these venerable Manhattan institutions.

One block north, at Forty-fifth Street, the Church of the Heavenly Rest was also being loaded on carts as debris. It, too, had fallen under the wrecker's ball for the sake of progress, the new church to be built at Fifth Avenue and Ninetieth Street. The following year, the minarets and filigreed stonework of Temple Emmanu-El at Forty-third Street toppled under the same pressure.

Twenty blocks to the north, the palace of "the" Mrs. Astor was about to be carried away, stone by stone, amid falling plaster and flying dust. Mrs. Astor's death in 1908 had ended an era, but the final knell for the

Golden Age came when her house crumbled under the wrecker's ball.

By 1924 the patrician citadel of hostelry, the Buckingham, just south of Saint Patrick's Cathedral, had come down, and in its place was erected the eleven-story Saks Fifth Avenue building, which still stands.

In 1925 Stanford White's Madison Square Garden on Madison Square was razed.

By 1926 one of the twin mansions of the Vanderbilt family was toppled, bringing down with it the cupids and gargoyles that adorned it. The William K. Vanderbilt chateau at the corner of Fifty-second Street and Fifth, scene of Alva Vanderbilt's costume ball, disappeared among clouds of dust rising from falling plaster. The Cornelius Vanderbilt house, then belonging to Alice G. Vanderbilt, the famed "Alice of the Breakers," was also scheduled for demolition. Bergdorf Goodman was soon to open on the site.

Across from the Plaza Hotel, the old Savoy was coming down, floor by floor, to make way for the Savoy Plaza, to be replaced, in 1965, by the General Motors Building. And the old Netherland was making way for the present Sherry-Netherland. Everywhere one looked, houses, mansions, churches, and landmarks were falling.

Along Millionaire's Row, on upper Fifth Avenue, the scene was devastating. Dozens of mansions were boarded up, and dozen of others were in process of demolition. In addition to the homes of Collis Huntington, William Rockefeller, Frank W. Woolworth, and Senator Clark, the list in 1926 alone included the following Fifth Avenue houses:

Ellen Bostwick	800 and 802
W. Emlen Roosevelt	804
Mrs. Hamilton Fish	810
Angelic L. Gerry	816
J. C. Hoagland	817
John W. Sterling	912
Samuel Thorn	914
Laura A. Palmer	922
Mrs. Rosina Hoppin	934

John W. Kaiser	953
Nicholas F. Brady	989
George Ehret	994
R. Fulton Cutting	1010
G. L. Hamersley	1030
Countess Leary	1032
James Cullman	1038
Edward F. Hutton	1107
Mrs. Dorothy Straight	1128
James Gerard	1134
Al Hyman	1138
Lloyd Price	1140

The reasons for the change were numerous. In 1913 the Sixteenth Amendment, empowering Congress to collect taxes on incomes, was passed, cramping the millionaire's style. Further, as space on Manhattan Island was now at a premium, building or maintaining a home on Fifth Avenue was like building a bonfire out of banknotes, spectacular but expensive.

And the social tenor of the avenue had changed in the decade prior to the war. Society had to contend with Pittsburgh steel barons Frick and Carnegie, copper baron Senator Clark, tinplate magnate Reid, and Charles T. Yerkes, the rapid-transit king—men who had earned their own wealth rather than inheriting it. As a result, many of the older families felt that Fifth Avenue had become nouveau riche and moved, consequently, to side streets in less conspicuous areas.

Society had also become nomadic. No longer was the Fifth Avenue "manse" a home. Summers were spent abroad or in Newport, and society wintered in Palm Beach, California, or the West Indies. The great houses were closed for a greater part of the year, except during the fall season, when the rich returned to their mansions for a two- or three-month stay. The "servant problem" had become acute; maintaining a fifty-room house required a staff of some twenty or thirty servants, far too many and too expensive to justify the short occupancy period. More and more people were moving into hotels or into smaller, more efficient apartments on

Park Avenue. This new life style enabled the rich to breeze into town at a minute's notice, put up in a hotel, and expect everything to go smoothly; in the old days, on the other hand, two or three weeks' notice had been needed for hiring a staff and putting a house in order. It no longer paid to keep a house on Fifth Avenue; it was easier, cheaper, and allowed one more freedom to dispense with it.

And so, with the dust of demolition in the air and social change so obvious, it began to be obvious that the days of the Waldorf-Astoria were numbered. And on December 21, 1928, at the height of the dizzy pace of the decade, there appeared on page one of the *New York Times* the inevitable headline: "Waldorf-Astoria Sold, Fifty Story Building to be Erected on Site." The story began, "The Waldorf-Astoria has been sold. On the site of this internationally known hotel, a center of American social, political and financial activities for two generations, will rise a fifty-story office building next summer."

The directors of the "Waldorf-Astoria" Realty Corporation, and Lucius Boomer, the president, held a news conference and released the following statement: "The Waldorf-Astoria Hotel, Astor Court and Astor Court Office Building have been sold to the Bethlehem Engineering Corporation. Delivery of the properties will be made next summer and the building will be demolished." The price paid was not revealed; however, the tab was estimated to be $20 million.

In his statement, Boomer further added: "While the Waldorf-Astoria still maintains its world wide prestige and an unimpaired volume of business, the great non-productive areas in the hotel, involving enormous taxation and operating costs, have become so burdensome a more profitable use of the site than for hotel purposes is indicated. This is the reason for the sale."

Another spokesman for the hotel indicated that the wide corridors and large public rooms on the ground floor were not in keeping with present-day hotel construction, that they used up valuable space without a return.

During the course of the news briefing, there were strong indications that the Waldorf-Astoria might be rebuilt on some other site. "We retain all rights to the name of the Waldorf-Astoria Hotel for future use," said Boomer—but questions that followed were met with "no comment." And so, within a year demolition was to begin, and a fabulous era in American social history would come to an end.

Within a few days, the *New York Times* wrote of the coming demise in an editorial:

ANOTHER LANDMARK GOING

Announcing the sale of the Waldorf-Astoria, Mr. Boomer declares that the former owners of the hotel "retain all rights to the name for future use." That is natural enough, and yet we wonder if they will ever actually use it for another hostelry. It is inextricably associated with the old hotel, and the memories of luxury and fashion which cluster about it. Men of leading [families] made their home there, and it was a mecca for thousands the country over who did not consider a visit to New York complete were they not able to find shelter under its roof and to enjoy the vicarious elegance of its parlors. "Waldorf-Astoria!" That bit of effusive orotund magnificently became the place. There was something almost onomatopoetic about it. When you looked at the haughty red pile you just knew this must be its name.

Shed a passing tear for the Waldorf if you will, but no more. There is no occasion for inordinate grief. It is not as if the hotel had been struck down in its prime, like some of our other landmarks, hardly built before they are in the wrecker's hands. It lived its life honorably and to the full. It met the exacting needs of one generation and must give way to the no less exacting needs of another. Spacious halls and high ceilings are, alas!, no longer the fashion. The high price of land has, in no slang sense, cramped our style. Where we used to dispose lavishly of yards, we must now husband inches. Such expansion as we are permitted is vertical, not horizontal. The office building that is to grow from the roots of the old hotel will be fifty stories high. Deep under ground will be "loading bays" for trucks—whoever heard of either when the Waldorf was built?—and a vast automobile garage. That is what the builder must save his space for nowadays. At least the community will be grateful to him if he is foresighted enough to do so, and in this way mitigate the congestion bred of his lofty spires.

The Empire State Building as a concept had yet to coalesce. A year later, the fifty-story building planned would give way to the grandiose plan to erect the tallest building in the world.

And so, in the spring of 1929, just six months before October's Black Friday stock market crash, which sent the world tailspinning into the Great Depression of the 1930s, the grand old Waldorf-Astoria Hotel entered the last few weeks of its existence. The newspapers were full of feature stories about its history and of its fabled guests. Of Li Hung-chang, the Chinese diplomat who arrived in New York clothed in yellow silk robes and was thought to have smoked opium in the lobby; of Albert and Elizabeth, king and queen of the Belgians; of the Prince of Wales; of General Pershing; and of the Bradley-Martin ball; of "Bet-a-Million" Gates; of Oscar and "Peacock Alley," and of every President from Grover Cleveland to Herbert Hoover. The nostalgia was so thick it could only be washed away by the thousands of tears shed by dewy-eyed, sentimental devotees of the old hotel.

On May 1, 1929, a gala dinner was presented that closed the doors of the old hotel forever. Toasts to a gaslit past were drunk with mineral water, as Prohibition was honored in the ballroom where champagne had bubbled forth from fountains of crystal and silver. After thirty-six years as queen of American hotels and as the center of the New York social scene, the hotel was about to be delivered first into the hands of the auctioneers and then the wreckers.

The dinner was held in the very same ballroom where Colonel Theodore Roosevelt had dined after his first election to the Presidency of the United States. Some seven hundred gentlemen, beaus of an earlier day, and their ladies gathered to sing the swan song. The ladies sat in the rococo balconies, almost hidden by the trailing arbutus and magnolia blossoms, in the manner of the past decades, when cigars were smoked after the ladies' departure. Oscar of the Waldorf had prepared a special menu, and when guests surreptitiously slipped silver spoons into their pockets, spoons engraved with the Waldorf-Astoria crest, waiters understood and made no objection. At the end of the evening, at 2:00 A.M., the guests sang "Auld Lang Syne," and thirty-six years of New York social history drew to a close.

Following the gala, the auction commenced as the owners disposed of over two and a half million dollars' worth of furnishings. Requests came in from all over the country for souvenir ashtrays, candelabra, cups and saucers, anything on which the Waldorf's emblem was emblazoned. The ballroom chairs, with their hand-painted Waldorf emblems, were especially prized. Literally hundreds of people wrote in from all corners of the country, bidding on the beds in which they had passed their wedding nights. However, perhaps the most bizarre request came directly to ex-Governor Alfred E. Smith, who was about to be named president of the Empire State Building Corporation. Mrs. Emily Smith Warner, daughter of the late Smith, reports that someone wanted the door to the room in which Ruth Snyder, the notorious Pig Woman, and Judd Gray had spent the night after the sensational murder of her husband in New Jersey.

On May 2 the 105 remaining guests who had retained their rooms during the hotel's last night moved to other hotels or to private apartments. The lights were turned out and the doors locked—and an era vanished.

3

The Empire State Building Rises

Even while the magnificent Waldorf-Astoria continued as the social center of New York City, a group of business leaders looked into the future and saw that the site was inevitably destined to become a throbbing center of business activity. As it had been the social focus in the residential life of early Manhattan, when the Astor mansion stood there; and as it had been the beautiful ideal of New York's Four Hundred, when the great mecca of the social world paraded under the huge mirrors of the Waldorf-Astoria, so it would crown the city with an imposing structure of commerce. The vision took on a more tangible aspect when the owners of the hotel decided to move to an uptown location over the railroad tracks of the New York Central Railroad, at Park Avenue and Fiftieth Street, where the present hotel stands.

The relocation of the hotel spurred this group of big money men into action. Most active among them was John Jacob Raskob, who had lifted himself out of the slums, up through the Du Pont empire, and eventually co-created General Motors. Coleman du Pont and Pierre S. du Pont, president of E. I. du Pont de Nemours, the chemical industry's leading empire, and the man who saved the empire for the family, and two lesser tycoons, Louis G. Kaufman and Ellis P. Earle, were also backers. Their dream was to build a skyscraper surpassing in its simple beauty any skyscraper ever designed, and meeting in its interior arrangements the most exacting requirements of the most critical tenant.

As their leader, they selected a man so well known to the public that his very presence placed the seal of integrity upon their undertaking. Although he had neither money nor business experience to contribute, Alfred E. Smith, ex-governor of New York State, was brought into the project by Raskob, who had been chairman of the Democratic National Committee of 1928, when Smith ran and lost the presidency against Republican Herbert Hoover. Both were staunch Catholics and together had weathered the brutality of the anti-Catholic attacks during the campaign, and when Smith returned to private life and needed a job, Raskob was there to give it to him. Smith was, at the time, chairman of the board of directors of the County Trust Company of New York and was—if not in Middle America, certainly in New York—a man of legendary magnetism, endeared to the common people as well as to the powerful elite. He served as the highly glamorous front man for the project, and was appointed president of Empire State, Incorporated, even while it was only a dream. With him came Robert C. Brown, who became vice-president of the corporation.

Raskob also handpicked the man to direct the renting campaign, and to create a tenant and public relations program. He selected H. Hamilton Weber, the young rental manager of the New York Central Building at 230 Park Avenue. Raskob had been a tenant in the Park Avenue building, and had gotten to know and admire Weber, having given him unexplained tasks to perform in connection with determining real estate values and analyzing rental conditions in certain parts of the city. At that time, unknown to Weber, Raskob and his associates were already negotiating for the Waldorf-Astoria site, and he was being considered for the post of rental director. Coincidentally, Weber had participated in the negotiations between the New York Central Railroad and the Waldorf-Astoria interests for the present Park Avenue site of the hotel.

Today Weber lives in suburban Short Hills, New Jersey, and is still active in the affairs of the Empire State Building. In a recent conversation he revealed exactly how Raskob had approached him on the matter of becoming rental agent. "One day, we were walking down Fifth Avenue when J. J. pointed at the old Waldorf-Astoria, looked at me, and said, 'Ham, you see that site over there?' I looked at him and nodded. Then he said to me, 'We're going to build the biggest and the highest building in the entire world over there. I want you to fill it up.' Needless to say, I was flabbergasted," said Weber.

With supreme confidence in their objectives, the Raskob–Du Pont group purchased the Waldorf-Astoria and the land underlying it. The entire procedure was done quietly, and few people knew what was in the wind until the official announcement of the sale was made. With that transaction the owners committed themselves to the stupendous task of making their vision come true. The die was cast, the work had begun— and nothing thereafter could be allowed to halt it. With a tremendous investment already made, plans had to go ahead full steam.

Having committed themselves and their money to the project, the group decided on the extent of the investment in the building itself. They estimated the cost of constructing one cubic foot and arrived at the conclusion that the building should be a structure of 36 million cubic feet. Thus, by simple arithmetic, the bulk of the Empire State Building was fixed.

On August 29, 1929, the economic skies were still bright. America was singing "Happy Days Are Here Again." Earlier in the year Admiral Byrd had discovered the South Pole, and Lucky Lindy had married Anne Morrow. Rudy Vallee was crooning "I'm Just a Vagabond Lover," and Thomas Wolfe had published his first novel, *Look Homeward Angel*, at the age of twenty-nine. Johnny Weissmuller retired after setting sixty-seven swimming records; he had yet to turn into Tarzan. On Valentine's Day Al

Capone's mob delivered a lethal card to the Moran gang in a garage in Chicago. Then, in August, the first public announcement of the Empire State Building was made. The news circled the world like lightning. The minds of men were thrilled, their imaginations stirred. Here was yet another daring adventure, another challenge to the ingenuity of man, another reaching for the heights. Who could foresee that two months later the stock market crash of Black Friday would send the world plummeting into the Great Depression of the 1930s?

The *New York Times* headlined the story on page one. "Smith to help build highest skyscraper. Ex-Governor heads group that will put up eighty story building on Waldorf site. Cost put at sixty million dollars," it read. The article went on to state that Alfred E. Smith would head the company to be incorporated to build the highest building in the world on the site of the Waldorf-Astoria Hotel. It said further:

The structure, to be known as the Empire State Building, will be an office building eighty stories high, and will cost, with the sixteen million paid for the site, more than sixty million dollars. It will occupy more than two acres of land with 200 feet on Fifth Avenue and 425 feet on Thirty-third and Thirty-fourth Streets.

Al Smith made the announcement in his suite at the Hotel Biltmore, in accordance with a promise made months before to newspaper reporters that he would announce his business plans as soon as he had determined them. The former governor said that supervision of the construction of the building and its management would be his main business. Although the governor made no mention of it in his announcement, it was said by friends that his salary as president of the building company would be about $50,000 a year.

And the world didn't have long to wait for the work to begin. Promptly following the first announcement, a motor truck drove through the wide door of the Waldorf-Astoria, the door at which had been received presidents and princes, heads of state and the uncrowned kings and queens of society. The truck, like a roaring invader, thrust its great bulk into the lobby, where surely such an intruder had never been seen before. It churned across the floor, then turned and roared down "Peacock Alley," down that proud corridor lined with gold mirrors and velvet draperies.

On the first of October, after the fittings and furnishings had been offered at auction, demolition was formally begun. Alfred E. Smith and John J. Raskob, representing the owning corporation, went to the roof of the hotel and dislodged the topmost stone of the cornice with crowbars. Then the wrecking crew, a seven-hundred-man army with derricks, compressors, and oxyacetylene burners went to work and demolished the hotel. Grand as it was, ornate as it had been, there was little demand for the ornaments in the hotel, and little use for the building materials. The copper roof and the steel frame were the only important parts of the hotel worth saving. The rest, as the structure came down under the sledges and the flaming torches of the wreckers, was carted off in motor trucks and loaded on barges. Five miles beyond Sandy Hook, New Jersey, the Waldorf-Astoria Hotel was dumped into the sea.

During the razing, the shock waves of Wall Street's Black Friday reverberated throughout the world. However, Raskob and company, who had vast investments to protect and whose retreat would have meant huge losses, bolstered their scheme by informing the public that now was the time to buy stock. In fact, the *New York Times* reported that Senator A. R. Robinson of Indiana had accused Raskob of being "psychologically" responsible for the stock market catastrophe. In December a $27 million loan from the Metropolitan Life Insurance Company was announced, and despite the bleak state of the American economy, the project moved ahead.

The problem of financing the construction was solved. However, there were also other problems, those of an architectural nature. The site measured about two acres, 83,860 square feet, but on only a quarter of this area could they build to any considerable height because of the strict zoning code, introduced after the construction of the massively proportioned Equitable Building on lower Broadway. It was required that buildings grow narrower as they rise, creating many "wedding cake" monstrosities in the city. (After 1961 the zoning laws were revised, granting more space on the higher floors of a building if they are set back from the street level.) On the Fifth Avenue frontage, for example, the law allowed buildings to rise sheer from the sidewalk only 125 feet, at which point a setback was required. Though they had bought two acres of land, the builders could build straight up on only half an acre, on approximately the center of the site. Thus, the law began to give some shape to that great building of 36 million cubic feet.

The problem of design was turned over to architects Robert H. Shreve, William F. Lamb, and Arthur Loomis Harmon, principals of the firm of Shreve, Lamb and Harmon. Definite limits in which they had to work were set—the size of the building, 36 million cubic feet; the sum available for construction; the size of the site; the element of time, only eighteen months from drawing board to completion and occupancy; and the requirements of the city zoning laws. All were facts, hard, unalterable facts, within which and around which the architects had to prepare their drawings. And there was one more limitation that the designers placed upon themselves, the requirement of beauty.

William Frederick Lamb, of the firm, set about to design the building. Born in Brooklyn on November 21, 1883, he was the son of William Lamb, a New York builder, and Mrs. Louise Wurster Lamb. He received his B.A. degree from Williams College in 1904 and then did graduate work at the Columbia University School of Architecture. Following that he went to Paris and studied at the Atelier Deglane, with a view toward taking his degree at the École des Beaux Arts. He received his diploma from the Beaux Arts in 1911.

Mrs. William F. Lamb, the widow of the architect, who lives in New York City, mentioned that despite the custom of the period to refer to others by their initials, Lamb was always referred to by everybody as Mr. Lamb. Even she, she said, could never quite call him Bill. "William, yes, but never Bill. He had a foreign aristocratic bearing and look about

The Great Portal—Fifth Avenu
showing Mr. Lamb's restrained eagle

him. His father had come from Scotland, and I expect he got it from him. He was not the least bit snobbish, but he was rather formal.

"When he received his degree from the Beaux Arts, he graduated sixth in his class, which was quite an accomplishment, considering that he spoke only rudimentary French. Shortly after that he bought a motorcycle and traveled the continent. When returning from Italy, he hit a wine cart and subsequently lost his leg. He remained in the hospital for nearly a year. This accident had a great deal to do with forming his career, as in World War I he couldn't join his friends in battle. It was then that he decided to move straight on into architecture and joined the firm of Carrere and Hastings."

Mrs. Lamb, in speaking of the influences that formed her husband's work, said that he was very fond of the French Romanesque as seen at Vezelay and Autun in France. "It is very clean and classical. The same went for his taste in music. He liked purity in music and was very sensitive to it. I think this shows up in the purity of line reflected in the design of the Empire State. He didn't like the Grand Central Building and that kind of ornate architecture. He always referred to it as the Little Nemo school of architecture. And eagles! He always had great difficulty with them, and was not very fond of them. You will notice that his eagles on the Empire State Building are very restrained."

As for the project, "he was profoundly relieved to have it back in 1929. In fact, it partially saved the firm from going under. He was pleased throughout the entire project, and was very happy with the way things went. Raymond Hood, one of the architects for Rockefeller Center, once said to him, 'Well, there's one thing you won't have to struggle with to make it look tall!' I do think that he thought the Empire State was his masterpiece. You know, when they added the television tower to the building, he was not very happy about that at all. And now with the suggested addition to the tower—my goodness, that would be like putting a neon sign on the facade of Saint Peter's Cathedral in Rome. He was particularly concerned about the suicides, and worked for many years to devise protection to keep people from jumping off.

"As for the inspiration for the design, a large pencil served. He was at the drawing board one day and set a large pencil on end. The clean soaring lines inspired him, and he modeled the building after it."

Lamb was a man of great taste. He abhorred the kitsch that later surrounded the building. Ashtrays, plates, paperweights, and the like in the shape of the Empire State Building were not to his liking. One time, shortly after the opening of the building, the Lambs received an invitation to the wedding of a daughter of one of Mr. Lamb's classmates. They lived in Columbus, Ohio, and Lamb said to Mrs. Lamb that he didn't think they needed to go, since he had not seen the man in twenty-five years. They decided to send a wedding present instead. Shortly after the wedding they received a letter from the bride; they had not as yet sent the wedding present. The letter read, "It was so nice of you to send it. There was no card, but we knew it was you because it was a lamp in the shape of the Empire State Building."

Sixteen times Lamb drew plans for the Empire State. And fifteen times changes were made in the topmost portion, and fifteen times the shape, arrangement, and appearance of the building were sketched, studied, altered, restudied, and rejected. Bit by bit, this succession of plans whittled away ells and wings, carved away buttresses, and scooped out whole blocks of floors. Finally "Plan K" came. Plan K is the Empire State Building as we know it today. The final setback requirements of the zoning law were applied, in one simple gesture, at the height of only five floors above the street. The entrance itself stands four floors high, the spacious lobby three. In the center are the groups of elevators, stairs, and provision for the essential services of the tower. The base, by itself an impressive building, is topped by a terrace, sixty feet broad, which sweeps back to the foot of the tower. From that point, separated from the surrounding buildings to assure perpetual light and air, the Empire State Building soars without a break for over one thousand feet to the eighty-sixth floor.

Actually, the building was designed from the top down. Since good engineering requires that the skeleton frame of the tower, the elevator shafts and pillars and foundations, must go through from top to bottom of the building, the shape of the tower determines the shape of the whole structure. Thus, the design of a typical floor in the tower became the first task of the architect. Not the foundation, nor the street level, but the eighty-sixth floor was the first plan completed.

In a series of articles that appeared in *Architectural Forum* in 1930 and 1931, William F. Lamb wrote the section entitled, "The General Design," in which he explained the problems he encountered and the solutions he arrived at:

An interesting development in the planning of present day office buildings is the change in the conception that the architect has of his work. The day that he could sit before his drawing board and make pretty sketches of decidedly un-economic monuments to himself has gone. His scorn of things "practical" has been replaced by an intense earnestness to make practical necessities the arma-ture upon which he moulds the form of his idea. Instead of being the intolerant aesthete, he is one of a group of experts upon whom he depends for the success of his work, for the modern large building with its complicated machinery is beyond the capacity of any one man to master, and yet he must, in order to control the disposition and arrangement of this machine, have a fairly accurate general knowledge of what it is all about. Added to this he must know how to plan his building so that it will "work" economically and produce the revenue for which his clients have made their investment.

In this spirit of cooperation with experts, the builder and engineer, the effort was made to solve the problem of the design of the Empire State. The program was short enough—a fixed budget, no space more than twenty-eight feet from window to corridor, as many stories of such space as possible, an exterior of limestone, and completion by May 1, 1931, which meant a year and six months from the beginning of the sketches. The first three of these requirements produced the mass of the building; and the latter two, the characteristics of its design.

In the first sketches an effort was made to develop the plan from studies, previously prepared for another owner, for a fifty-story building of the loft type on the same site. These sketches show the elevators placed at right angles to the main axis of the building. The elevator groups "drop off" in sequence, an arrangement that forced the tower far back from the Fifth Avenue front. The "loft" type plan was indented to introduce light into the deep space, but this idea produced many dark corners, and gave too much volume for the height desired. The plan of the tower was also a relic of the previous scheme, and when additional elevators were added, there resulted a floor plan that was not capable of good subdivision. This plan was therefore abandoned.

In the meantime, a preliminary investigation was being carried on by the group of experts that had been formed to inquire into the many and difficult technical problems that had to be solved before any serious work could begin. This group included Bassett Jones for the elevators, H. G. Balcom for the steel frame, Henry C. Meyer for the heating and ventilating, and Fred Brutschy for the plumbing.

The elevator system was one of the keys to both the general arrangement of the plan and the height to which the building could rise. The critical point that determined the number of cars that could be provided for was at about the thirtieth floor, where, legally, the tower begins, for with the area of this floor restricted by the zoning requirements to one-quarter of the size of the property, there was a limited amount of space that could be used for "utilities" and still have adequate space to rent. Study, therefore, concentrated on this portion of the building, to find the most economical shape and arrangement of the floor, giving at the same time the greatest number of elevators. The elevator banks were placed parallel to the main axis of the building in four groups, and the stairs, toilets, and shafts were located between the unused banks. The elevator runs were studied so that these utilities could easily be transferred when the various banks came into or went out of service, a study that resulted in the adoption of the principle that the form of the shaft should be much more nearly a square than that shown on the previous schemes, which would also, to a large extent, simplify the problem of wind resistance.

The great height contemplated made the problem of wind bracing extremely important, especially in the narrower dimensions of the property. It was highly desirable that all the columns should, in addition to carrying through vertically, also be in line horizontally in both directions, but more especially in the narrower sense, producing a complete gridiron. This principle was adhered to until it was found that the columns became so large at the bottom that they could not be placed in front of the tower elevator shafts, which made it necessary to substitute two bays for three in the longer side of the tower in that portion of the building.

At the same time, consultation with Meyer and Brutschy determined in a general way the size and location of ventilation and pipe shafts, which were such that they became a very important consideration in the general scheme. Conferences with the builders, Starrett Brothers and Eken, fixed the general speed program and types of building construction.

The principles established by these cooperative investigations, which covered a period of four weeks, together with the owner's requirements, now formed the complete program. The "parti" was arrived at in two hours, the evening before a meeting of the owner's corporation. An all-night "charrette" produced the next day a series of five or six of the essential plans, an elevation, a perspective, and a fairly accurate tabulation of rentable areas and cubes. It is interesting to compare these plans with later ones after they had been worked out in detail.

The logic of the plan is very simple. A certain amount of space in the center, arranged as compactly as possible, contains the vertical circulation, toilets, shafts, and corridors, and surrounding this is a perimeter of office space twenty-eight feet deep. The sizes of the floors diminish as the elevators decrease in number. In essence there is a pyramid of nonrentable space surrounded by a greater pyramid of rentable space, a principle modified, of course, by practical consideration of construction and elevator operation. The four groups of high-rise elevators are placed in the center of the building, with the low-rise groups adjoining on the east and west sides so that, as these drop off, the building steps back from the long dimension of the property to approach the square form of the shaft, with the result that, instead of being a tower, set upon a series of diminishing setbacks prescribed by the zoning law, the building becomes all tower, rising from a great five-story base.

While these sketches fixed the general mass of the building, its height had not yet been fully determined. Two very important factors were to make this decision: elevators and budget. Jones, therefore, commenced an accurate determination of the elevators, which he could now do with the sketch plans and the floor-by-floor areas, and Starrett Brothers and Eken, for the purpose of determining how high the building might be carried within the budget, made a careful approximate estimate based on these same sketches and an outline specification. It was a coincidence that both arrived at a limit of eighty stories, plus five floors of penthouse.

At this point, with the general plan and the mass of the building determined, there entered the last and perhaps the most important item in the owner's program—speed of construction. The development of the window and spandrel design, although worked out through an ardent desire to get rid of reveals, inadequate and useless in a building of such height, was the solution to the problem of the rapid building of the limestone walls, and the scheme of the vertical strips and mullions of polished steel, which give the building its characteristic appearance, was evolved to effect, in a simple manner, a proper junction between wall and window. The elimination of all shelf angles and other special steel supports for the stone piers made it possible to prepare the steel drawings and proceed with fabrication before the design and fenestration of the exterior were determined in detail, providing an opportunity to study the window treatment with great care; many small-scale models were made in an effort to visualize what the effect would be. These studies proved the necessity (if the time schedule didn't) of handling the stonework with utmost simplicity, so it would become merely a background for the applied metal and glass. It was only in the lower stories that some detail was introduced, in the pier caps and the flanking half columns of the main entrance.

It would be interesting to speculate on the influence this speed program had upon the design. Hardly a detail was issued without having been thoroughly analyzed by the builders and their experts, then adjusted and changed to meet every foreseen delay. Choice of interior marbles was limited to those which could be obtained in time to be fabricated and set, and men were sent to the quarries abroad to get this information first hand. Rose Famosa and Estrallante were selected for the great entrance halls—10,000 square feet of marble devoid of detail, depending for the effect entirely on their highly interesting color and veining—with 300,000 square feet of Hauteville and Rocheron for the elevator lobbies and corridors on the office floors—quantity production—sawn, "coped," and polished.

As far as possible, hand work was done away with, for in quantity production, with thousands of pieces of each material identical in shape and size, the delay would have been disastrous. Windows, spandrels, steel mullions, and stone, all fabricated in various parts of the country, were designed so they could be duplicated in tremendous quantity with almost perfect accuracy, then brought to the building and put together almost like an automobile on the assembly line. The limestone ashlar was made in such dimensions that it could be handled on ordinary material hoists within the building, trundled by baggage trucks to the perimeter of the floor, and from there dropped by cable into its place in the wall between the steel jamb pieces, which were already set.

The adaptation of the design to conditions of use, construction, and speed of erection was kept to the fore throughout the development of the drawings of the Empire State. Whatever "style" it may be was the result of a logical and simple answer to the problems set by the economic and technical demands of this unprecedented program.

Before a spadeful of earth was turned for the Empire State, even before a stone of the old Waldorf was dislodged in the demolition operations, the Empire State Builing was built, complete—on paper. The architects and the general contractor, the firm of Starrett Brothers and Eken, knew exactly how many beams and of what lengths, even how many rivets and bolts would be needed. They determined how many windows the building would have, how many blocks of limestone, and of what shapes and sizes; how many tons of aluminum and stainless steel; how many tons of cement and of mortar.

Then orders were given to the steel mills in Pittsburgh. Cement and lime were ordered from upstate New York. Quarrymen in Indiana began to cut limestone. Marble was ordered from Germany and France, lumber from the Pacific Coast, and hardware from New England's factories. Every order was exact and complete: the quantity was specified; the size and length and weight were clearly stated. Even the precise day of future delivery was indicated.

If all the materials required for the project had come to the building site in a single shipment, a train fifty-seven miles long would have been required, and when its locomotive entered New York City, the caboose at the rear of the train would have stopped in Bridgeport, Connecticut. The 10 million bricks needed would have taken one bricklayer, working a seven-day schedule, twenty-five years to lay. Approximately 200,000 cubic feet of stone were quarried, transported to New York and placed on the façade. In one shipment, this Indiana limestone would have required a train of over 400 flat cars. Some 6,500 windows were needed to flood the farthest corners of the building with daylight.

Rubber-covered wire cable for the elevators totaled 1,172 miles, enough to reach down the entire East Coast of the United States, from New York City to Jacksonville, Florida. Seventy-five miles of main water pipe were ordered to be laid under the floors and in the walls, along with 50 miles of radiator pipe for heating. For the outer walls, 730 tons of aluminum and stainless steel were ordered; 400 fire hose connections were provided for, to give the building's tenants the protection of a completely self-contained fire department; 60,000 pairs of office telephone cable for 3,000 trunk line switchboards and 5,000 station telephones were put in place under the floor in doubly armored ducts. For power and light, 2 million feet of electric wires was specified, equal to nearly 380 miles in total length, the distance from New York to Buffalo.

Since time was of the essence, an overlapping schedule for raising the new building was set up. October 1929 to February 1930 was the period of demolition on the schedule. January 1930 to March 1930 for excavation, then March 1930 to September 1930 for structural steel; June 1930 to December 1930 for exterior masonry; May 1930 to January 1931 for metal window frames; and May 1930 to February 1931 for mail chutes and elevators, with June 1930 to February 1931 for interior partitions and March 1931 to occupancy for painting and revolving doors.

If this schedule could be maintained, and it was, the Empire State Building would become the grand champion in the city's favorite architectural sport, sky racing. Twenty years before, Metropolitan had leaped into the sky and crowned the city with its 700-foot Wall Street tower. However, when Frank Woolworth had approached Metropolitan for a loan and been refused, in a fit of pique, he commissioned Cass Gilbert to build his Gothic cathedral on City Hall Park, completed in 1913. The Woolworth Building, at 792 feet, stood as the tallest building in the city for sixteen years. During the twenties, the competition began again, with the Bank of Manhattan Building at 927 feet appearing to be the front runner. Meanwhile, however, in midtown, Walter Chrysler's structure was rising. It was not considered a serious contender, but in a surprise finish a finial spire, secretly put together inside the building, was elevated through the dome. At 1,046 feet the Chrysler Building not only one-upped the Bank of Manhattan, but was 62 feet taller than the Eiffel Tower, making it the tallest building in the world. However, the Chrysler Building's reign was brief, for even as it was opening in 1930, the Empire State was already under construction.

Before the construction began, the Empire State was scheduled to be a structure of eighty-six floors topped by an observation tower. That would make it 1,050 feet high, giving it nine more rentable floors than the Chrysler Building, but only a 4-foot advantage over the Chrysler's surprise spire. One day, when Raskob was studying the plaster model of the final version, he exclaimed, "What this building needs is a hat!" He had in mind the construction of a mast to moor dirigibles, thinking they would be the forthcoming mode of international travel. And so, in December of 1929, he projected the 200-foot mooring mast for dirigibles. The *New York Times* carried an announcement on December 12:

A mooring tower for dirigibles with a built in landing platform for trans-Atlantic passengers will tower 1300 feet, a quarter of a mile, above Fifth Avenue. . . . Thus, the structure will be not only the tallest building in the world, but the first to be equipped for a future age of transportation that is now only a dream of pioneers in aviation.

Al Smith stated that the dirigibles would be warped to the mast by an electrical winch, much as an ocean liner is warped to its pier. A ship once moored can swing in the breeze; the passengers would go down a gangplank to the elevator in the tower. He added that

the directors of the Empire State, Inc., believe that in a comparatively short time the Zeppelin airships will establish trans-Atlantic, transcontinental and trans-Pacific lines, and possibly a route to South America from the port of New York. Building with an eye to the future, it has been determined to erect this mooring tower to land people directly on Thirty-fourth Street and Fifth Avenue after their ocean trip, seven minutes after the airship connects with the mast.

The following day, Smith left for Washington to discuss the proposed airship mooring mast with navy engineers. The directors had conferred with engineers and officials of the Goodyear Zeppelin Corporation of Akron, Ohio. Commander Jerome C. Hunsaker, vice-president of the company and president of a recently formed airship transport company, said:

This mooring mast is perfectly feasible. It will require some revision of the plans for the new building and certain engineering changes in the entire steel structure to the foundations to make provision for the stresses that would be set up by a thousand-foot airship swinging in the wind and held to the building by a single connection.

Down in Lakehurst, New Jersey, at the United States Naval Air Station, officers had expressed much interest in the proposed mooring mast, but pointed out that a huge airship almost as long as the building would be tail swinging in the winds, and vertical air currents set up by the high buildings and intervening streets would require continual trimming to keep on anything like an even keel. When Smith arrived in Washington, he met receptive ears.

Many other people, however, were skeptical. Raskob was warned that dirigibles couldn't possibly be moored atop the building, but he insisted that the structure have a spectacular and unique feature in order to ignite the public's imagination and bring business to the Thirty-fourth Street area. The *New York Telegram* jested, "If you know how to hold down the tail of a dirigible, former Governor Alfred E. Smith may give you a job. . . ." But in fact the idea did catch on, and later, when the mast was constructed, did capture the public's imagination and attention. There were two moorings of blimps within a few months after the building was formally opened. On September 15, 1931, a privately owned dirigible tied up in a forty-mile wind for a scant three minutes. Two weeks later a Navy blimp idled long enough to produce a headline in the *New York Times:* "Blimp Lands Papers on Empire State Building." During this attempt at docking, an updraft almost upended the craft and nearly swept away celebrities attending the historic affair. When water ballast was dumped from the blimp, pedestrians several blocks away were drenched and perplexed by the downpour from a cloudless sky.

The mooring mast idea was ultimately abandoned and Raskob's "hat" gradually fattened into a hollow tower with a second observation deck and gave the completed Empire State 102 stories and a height of 1,250 feet.

As 1929 turned into 1930, the nation found itself sinking deeper and deeper into depression. Before the year was out, apple sellers were huddled on frozen street corners and hundreds of banks went bankrupt as people panicked to withdraw savings. Still, some people had money. Three and a half million new cars were sold, and miniature golf boomed into a $125 million business. Jean Harlow's screen shenanigans diverted people, and Edward G. Robinson snarled in *Little Caesar,* ushering in an era of gangster flicks. Sinclair Lewis became the first American novelist to win a Nobel Prize, and Bobby Jones scored a grand slam. On January 12, 1930, the observation roof at the 1,050-foot level of the Empire State was announced. The *New York Times* wrote:

From a vantage point more than 1,000 feet above the heart of Manhattan, the vast panorama of the metropolitan district will be unfolded to the view of persons on the observation promenade of the Empire State Building when that eighty-five story office skyscraper is completed next year.

Al Smith further announced that several thousand square feet of space would be provided for observation purposes on the roof of the structure. He further stated that the platform would be two hundred feet higher than the one on the Eiffel Tower in Paris.

Then, about a week later, on January 22, 1930, even before the demolition of the Waldorf was completed, the excavation for the building commenced. The sub-basement level of the building averaged about 30 feet below street level, requiring exceptionally large quantities of rock and earth to be removed. Footings for 210 steel and concrete columns went down to bedrock. These column footings were to support the structure, with some of those in the tower structure to carry as much as 5,000 tons of weight each. Like all tall buildings, the Empire State had to be set upon the firmest foundation, the basic rock that is the earth itself. Only where the rock is near the surface can towers soar skyward, for they need a base from which to spring. It is this underlying stratum of granite which makes Manhattan's skyline possible.

The Empire State especially needed this unyielding foundation. With its great height and its enormous projected weight—303,000 tons of steel, stone, and materials—only Mother Earth could be trusted for sure support. And at the site, bedrock was near. The building reaches down only two floors, 33 feet below the sidewalk. There it stands, the base of its columns bedded deep in the stratum of granite that is the core of the earth.

If you wonder if even bedrock can support so vast a burden, if some day perhaps the bedrock may grow weary of the load and give way, geologists and engineers assure us that this can never happen. Geologists affirm that bedrock cannot yield or slip. Engineers report that when the Empire State foundations were excavated down to bedrock, the weight of earth and stone removed was equal to three-quarters of the weight of the building itself. The burden placed on bedrock by the towering height of the Empire State is just slightly greater than the load that was being supported naturally. The building, then, is no new load placed on the bedrock. Instead, the inert load of earth and stones put there by nature has been dug away and replaced by a useful load in the form of the building. On March 6, 1930, the *New York Times* announced that the excavation was completed.

On March 8 workmen were ready to set steel, to begin work on the skeleton of the building, but Al Smith, in tribute to his Irish ancestry, and with the savvy of a first-rate publicist, requested that the ironworkers delay the start until St. Patrick's Day on March 17. On that date the erectors moved ahead with demonic speed, setting construction records that are still unequaled. The first steel piers were sunk. Nearly 57,000 tons of steel went into the skeleton, about three times as much as the Chrysler Building, and enough to make a double-track railroad all the way to Baltimore.

The schedule was and remains mind boggling. Steel was poured and set into girders in Pittsburgh. The girders were then sped by freight train to a waterfront supply yard in New Jersey, from whence they were trucked to the Fifth Avenue site, lifted in bundles on cables, and set in place.

The excavation for the Empire State Building.

The first five stories are erected, as seen
from the corner of Fifth Avenue and 34th Street.
Notice the old boulevard lamps atop the street sign.

During construction.
Twenty-five stories up, as seen from
the corner of Fifth Avenue and 34th Street.

65

66

(Above) The Empire State Building reaches up forty stories.
(Right) Two dirigibles approach the unfinished Empire State Building in 1931.
The mooring mast atop the building was planned as a port for the flying behemoths,
however, the plan proved unfeasible and the mast was abandoned. UPI.

Steel was in place 80 hours after being put in the furnaces in Pittsburgh. The metal skeleton was completed in just 23 weeks. There was one innovation in construction, born of an accident during the construction of the Chrysler building, in which a derrick operator had dropped his bundle of steel after being knocked unconscious by a flying brick: 16 electrically driven derricks were equipped with automatic hoists. Despite this safety precaution, however, the *New York Daily News* reported upon the completion of the building that 14 men were killed in various accidents during the raising of the building, as compared with one during the Chrysler construction.

When the steel arrived at the site, fitting-up and raising gangs hoisted the material up to the riveting gangs at the ever-heightening top. Then a heater, a bucker-up, a sticker-in, and two riveters secured the girders with machines. At the peak of the construction, 38 riveting gangs were working, with 300 steelworkers interchanging their posts.

The exterior stages of the operation could be seen from the street below. The dark mass of steel squares near the top soon gave way to the gray stone facing, lined with the shining strips of metal that formed the outstanding feature of the façade decoration. The first four or five stories above the street were still open, but even as the sidewalk superintendents watched, derrick slings carried long slabs of stone facing to the proper floors and began to enclose them. Looking up one could see the top derricks swinging out over the street, and the riveters could be heard but seldom seen. Double-wheeled trucks moved through three gateways leading to the humming confusion of the first floor.

Inside was a forest of concrete-covered piers. The activity was staggering to behold. Truckloads of brick were unloaded with a roar, as each truck tipped its load and sent it thundering down through the floor into a basement hopper. Tiles were unloaded more gingerly, by hand. Sheet-iron metal parts, bales of wire and coils of cable, sand and cinders, lumber and pipe arrived. Each was unloaded in a special corner of the block-wide

The tower nears completion.

Lewis W. Hine's photographs of the rising of the building.

floor, soon to be sent shooting up in the elevators to the floor where each was needed.

More than 3,000 men worked on the project daily, among them 225 carpenters, 290 bricklayers, 384 derrick men, 285 structural steel men, 249 elevator installers, 105 electricians, 192 plumbers, and 194 heating and ventilating men. Many others—trade specialists, inspectors, checkers, foremen, clerks, and water boys—worked as well. Even the dust on the planked wooden floor where the trucks arrived required men to settle it with water from watering cans.

The press was fascinated by the project and heaped praise on the steel-workers, calling them "the poet builders" and the "sky boys who ride the ball to the 90th floor and higher, and defy death to the staccato chattering of a pneumatic riveting-hammer." In May of 1931 the *Literary Digest* said:

Like little spiders they toiled, spinning a fabric of steel against the sky. Crawl-ing, climbing, swinging, swooping—weaving a web that was to stretch farther heavenward than the ancient Tower of Babel, or than all the elder towers of the modern Babel, as Manhattan has sometimes been tagged. Up there where "Bryant Park is a pancake" and as the *New Yorker* put it, "and the Statue of Liberty something to throw at a cat."

Lewis W. Hine was the pictorial historian of the building. A camera-man, some of whose stunning photographs of skyscraper builders in action are reproduced on the following pages, Hine had to learn to be a "spider" as well, but a watchful one, who smuggled his camera to all kinds of dizzy perches. The *New York Post* called his document on film

a saga of the men who, outlined against the sky on dizzy heights, fuse the iron of their nerves with the steel of the girders they build into modern cities. What Carl Sandburg has done for the Age of Steel in his poetry, Lewis W. Hine has tried to do pictorially.

The *Literary Digest* went on:

These pictures make it easy to understand the speed and skill with which modern sky-scrapers are erected. For the men who appear tiny as flies to the spectators in the streets beneath are shown here as muscular, clear-eyed, poised and self-confident creatures whom Lysippus or Phidias would have delighted to model in imperishable marble.

The *New York Evening Post* said of Hine's photograph entitled "Icarus," "One of the pictures which has attracted attention is of a workman swinging out from the building at a terrifying height, to which Mr. Hine has given the poetic title of 'Icarus.' The name suggested by the fact that the figure expresses the sense of flight."

In photographing workers on the mooring mast, over 1,000 feet above the streets, Hine was swung out over Fifth Avenue in a specially adapted basket. "Growing up with a building this way is like the account of the strong boy who began lifting a calf each day so that when they had both reached maturity he could shoulder the bull," said the photographer to a *Survey Graphic* reporter, who continued:

Hine is full of interesting information that he has picked up on his way up, such as that the girders were in place 80 hours after they were made in Pittsburgh . . . but he is most of all interested in the actual human beings he is photographing; he calls these workmen "the spirit of the skyscraper."

He is full of admiration for the nonchalant way in which they defy the law of gravitation. "These experiences," he says, "have given me a new zest of high adventure, and, perhaps, a different note in my pictorial interpretation of industry."

The workers represented the "melting pot" of America. A multitude of ethnic backgrounds, both union and nonunion men, worked astoundingly quickly on the building. Colonel Starrett, the builder, wrote, "The first column was set on April 7, 1930 and twenty-five weeks later over 57,000 tons of steel had been topped out. . . . 87 stories above the sub-basement level, 12 days ahead of schedule."

(*Pages 74–82*), Lewis W. Hine's photographs of the "sky boys" have been
likened to Walt Whitman's poetry in that they visually sing the praises of the robust
and dynamic quality of the men who made America. The photographer spent
many days climbing around on the upper reaches of the building during
construction, to document the labor of the men who built the building.

By September two topping-out celebrations were held. At the street level Al Smith laid the cornerstone. A crowd of 5,000 persons, half of whom were workers on the building, swarmed around Smith as he manipulated a silver trowel, cementing the 4,500-pound semicircular stone into place. The Swedish granite block, hardest and heaviest of any species of granite, was $2\frac{1}{2}$ feet thick and 6 feet in diameter, with a highly polished block surface.

A copper box, placed within the stone, contained a history of the building and the company erecting it. Also placed in the box were samples of the coinage and paper currency of 1930, in all denominations from a penny to a hundred-dollar bill; photographs of the officers of the building company, the architects, and contractors; and a rag-paper edition of the *New York Times* of September 9, 1930.

Facing a battery of cameras, the former governor, himself a member of the bricklayers' union, spoke briefly of the history of the site, while scores of workers perched perilously on steel beams and scaffolding above him shouted down friendly taunts. He said, "Since the advent of the movie camera, the radio and other means of communicating sound, the laying of a cornerstone of a public building today becomes somewhat of a photographic gallery performance. In the copper box here are certain articles of value indicating the trend of the time. If this building is ever demolished to make way for a greater building the people of that day can read pretty accurately the history of this day."

In replying to humorous criticism and remarks on his masonry skills from the workers, one of whom asked if there was any chance of putting the Eighteenth Amendment in the copper box, Smith replied, "So that there will be no mistake or misunderstanding about it, I declare, and firmly, that I have a right to use this trowel as a member of the union. My dues are all paid and I have my card in my office at 200 Madison Avenue."

Just nine days later the second topping-out ceremony occurred, as workers raised the American flag 1,048 feet above Fifth Avenue. The steel frame of the Empire State Building was completed. On November

(Overleaf) Lewis W. Hine's photo of Lower Manhattan at night, as seen from the unfinished heights of the Empire State Building.

22, another flag was raised, symbolizing the placing of the last piece of steelwork in the dirigible mooring mast atop the structure.

After the steel setters had completed their work, other crews swarmed in on their heels. Stairways rose through the skeleton, then electric cables and piping. Down on the lower floors, plastering was in process even before the roof was made tight. The concrete floor arches quickly followed the steel. Colonel Starrett wrote:

Early in October, 1930, the arches of the eighty-sixth floor were completed . . . about three million square feet of arches had been set. These arches required 62,000 cubic yards of anthracite cinder concrete and nearly three million feet of reinforcing mesh. As soon as this work had been thoroughly organized above the sixth floor, the stone setting and outside wall construction progressed at the rate of one story a day. All stonework except a few ornamental features around the lower floors were completely set in 113 days.

The construction went forward with absolute precision. On each floor, as the steel frame climbed higher, a miniature railroad was built, with switches and cars, to carry supplies. A perfect timetable was published each morning. At every minute of the day, the builders knew what material was going up on each of the elevators, to which height it would rise, and which gang of workers would use it. On each floor the operators of every one of the small trains of cars knew what was coming up and where it would be needed. Down below, in the streets, the drivers of the motor trucks worked on similar schedules. They knew, each hour of every day, whether they were to bring steel beams or bricks, window frames or blocks of stone. The moment of their departure from the storage place, the length of time allowed for moving through traffic, and the precise moment of arrival at the site of the building, all were calculated, scheduled, and fulfilled with absolute precision. Trucks did not wait, derricks and elevators did not swing idle, men did not wait. So perfect was the planning that workmen scarcely had to reach for what they needed next.

The care and feeding of the army of workers was a problem in itself. When the lunch whistle blew, five mobile cafeterias began shuttling up and down the scaffolding. For forty cents, and with no time lost, a man could sit on a girder and down two sandwiches, coffee or milk, and pie. Ten miles of temporary pipes were laid in the steel skeleton to provide drinking water for the workers, and a modern hospital, complete with an emergency operating room and staff of physicians and nurses, was installed in the broad base of the building and maintained until completion.

In the meantime, the world sank deeper and deeper into the Great Depression, and despite an announcement by Al Smith in January that rentals were active, people began to refer to the building as Smith's Folly, or "The Empty State Building," which, in fact, according to Mrs. Emily Smith Warner, is how the great Al himself often referred to it. On March 25, 1931, the *New York Times* editorialized on the subject in a piece entitled "Everest on Fifth Avenue."

America's tallest skyscraper lifts its 1,248 feet of office space and mooring mast to the clouds at a time when American business is believed to be still "scraping the bottom." Between the present low of our economic life and the unprecedented "high" of the Empire State Building at Fifth Avenue and Thirty-fourth Street, there is a connection. They are trough and crest of the wave rhythm of the nation's economic life. The dozens and scores of pinnacles that have pierced the skies over Manhattan in the last half dozen years, towers for doing business in and towers for living in, are the permanent notation of a great surge of prosperity. The tide itself once so often recedes. The towers are there to testify to the vast energy that threw them upward and that is certain to reassert itself after the necessary retirement. In the operations of the economic cycle, men always overreach themselves, from the temporary viewpoint. For a while the receding tide leaves these ambitious monuments high and dry. Then the waves begin to lap forward again, the tempo grows swifter, the crest rises higher, and in due course of time a new release of energy begins to throw upward new projects, new dreams and new towers.

Will the Empire State be transcended in the city's next building boom? Prophecy about this country is even more hazardous an occupation than elsewhere. On grounds of public policy, the critics of the skyscraper are beginning to make themselves heard. The problem of traffic congestion is, in large measure,

(*Overleaf*) Looking south to the Battery during construction.

the creation of the monster office building. The owners of the Empire State advertise the fact that three of their lower floors just rented by a great corporation have an area equal to that of a twenty-two story office building on a plot 100 by 100. The Empire's central tower has a smaller base than the main structure; yet with that allowance, the whole building must be equal to a flock of perhaps a dozen twenty-two-story buildings. We have already learned by experience what such a building, when fully occupied, does to movement in the adjacent streets.

There is also said to be an argument from bookkeeping against unlimited heights. Beyond a certain point the cost of building and running elevators is said to be approaching the prohibitive. Another practical argument derives from the time required to erect a giant building and equip it for occupancy. Even with all our rapid-construction methods, this is a matter of years, involving interest charges on enormous investments without return. Merely to fill up a giant building to its tenant capacity is generally assumed to be a matter of many months. The cynic might thus say that the chief argument against still higher and bigger business structures and hotels is that by the time a new building begins to pay the next business recession will be upon us.

There is an argument also from Beauty. The splendor and lift of New York's tallest pinnacle is such as to make the most hardened inhabitant catch his breath. Should there be many of these topless towers, if Americans are to retain any capacity at all for awe—and humility?

On April 11, 1931, the announcement of completion and formal opening were made. The building was completed—and only 28 percent rented. In the book *Empire State, A Pictorial Record of Its Construction*, by Vernon H. Bailey, Colonel Starrett said of the completion:

And now that this vast undertaking has been completed within a year from the setting of the first columns of the tower, not only the men who directed the work administratively, but all of the craftsmen whose skill and energy made possible the swift accomplishment, can take pride in the carrying out of this great enterprise. No man can say what is the greatest building undertaking ever accomplished. No comparison can be drawn between the efforts expended in constructing the pyramids and those put forth in the construction of Empire State. Neither can time elements be compared. Moreover, it would be presumptuous to assume that the construction of Empire State even measurably approaches what may be humanity's undertaking in the development of great metropolitan structures. However, all of the men who had to do with the building of Empire State may take full satisfaction in the feeling that this great structure, both in the organization of its management and speed of performance, is probably the greatest attainment in metropolitan construction of our time.

Although on the surface Starrett's pride may seem to be a bit overblown, nonetheless the Empire State Building still holds the record for the fastest rising major skyscraper ever built anywhere.

4

Al Smith's Big Party

Saturday, May 1, 1931, was the red-letter day everyone had been waiting for. The sky was crystal clear, the weather made to order. At exactly 11:15 A.M., $52 million worth of Empire State Building was formally opened. And in true Smithian fashion, the great ex-governor pulled out all stops. Combining the best features of David Belasco and Phineas T. Barnum with a few of his own touches, he threw a spectacular party to celebrate the opening. It was a joyous occasion and a glittering function, all reflecting the pride Smith had in the magnificent structure he had supervised as it rose, story by story, from the historic corner of Fifth Avenue and 34th Street to its massive height of 1,248 feet, a pride surpassed only by his feelings about his tenure as governor of New York State. Indeed, no other office building in the history of the city, before or since, had such a glorious debut. Of course, his guests that day, and subsequently over 40 million people, were treated to perhaps the most breathtaking view on earth.

The principals included Smith himself; the President of the United States, Herbert Hoover; the governor of the state of New York, Franklin Delano Roosevelt; the mayor of New York City, James J. Walker; Robert

H. Shreve, representing the architectural firm of Shreve, Lamb and Harmon, as well as Paul Starrett, representing the construction company, and many workmen speaking for their various crafts. Tributes and good wishes poured in from all over the world. However, it was Smith's grandchildren, Miss Mary Adams Warner and Master Arthur E. Smith, Jr., who really stole the show.

The opening got under way precisely on schedule at exactly 11:15 A.M., but for hours before that, crowds had been jamming into the Fifth Avenue and Thirty-fourth Street area. Two hundred invitations had been extended for the luncheon by the ex-governor, and without those nicely engraved squares of white, anybody who tried to crash the gate was distinctly out of luck. As it turned out 350 guests arrived, because prominent New Yorkers had asked and obtained permission to be accompanied by their wives or other members of their families. There were a great variety of policemen on hand—ordinary cops in blue uniforms, plainclothes police, state troopers, private detectives, and some members of the militia as well.

While crowds milled and pushed, to try to get a glimpse of Smith, and while police spurred up and down the avenue, hustling along automobiles that had a tendency to linger in front of the building, and while the invited guests were being shooed into the back door of the building, the Thirty-fourth Street door, Al Smith and his two grandchildren, Mary and Arthur, were standing right square in front of the main entrance on Fifth Avenue, the entrance that led into the great central corridor of the building. Both Al and the children were rather impatient for action, with the children dancing around in wild excitement. Photographers created a psychedelic light show with their flash bulbs as Al posed for hundreds of pictures. Waving his jet-black derby, the perfect accessory for his morning coat and striped pants, he received tremendous applause and cheers from the onlookers.

Finally, somebody who had kept an eye on the time approached the ex-governor and informed him that it was 11:15. "All right kids, get to it," said Smith. Across the main entrance was a broad red, white, and blue ribbon, Mary and Arthur, armed with scissors, were supposed to snip the ribbon. However, with all the excitement, they couldn't quite manage it. They slashed away as the crowds chuckled, until finally Smith grasped the middle of the stubborn ribbon and ripped it from its place. Then the police opened the doors, and Mary and Arthur, prodded by their illustrious ancestor, stepped, slightly timidly, over the threshold into the grand pink marble corridor, officially the first persons, outside of administrative forces and workmen, to enter the building. They skipped and danced down the corridor, the excited five-year-old Arthur in light blue and Mary in apple green. Just behind them walked Mr. and Mrs. Alfred E. Smith and a family party of their sons and daughters and their various in-laws. After them came Father Francis Duffy and William F. Kenney, a friend of the ex-governor.

Alfred E. Smith and his family at the opening of the Empire State Building, May 1, 1931. UPA

Smith guided his grandchildren to a position directly in front of the information desk in the main corridor, under the striking picture of the building itself rendered in stainless steel. There was a further wait while cameras clicked and flashbulbs popped.

Meanwhile down in Washington, the President of the United States, Herbert Hoover, was waiting for the hands of the clock to point to 11:30. Presently 11:30 came. The President pushed a button and the great main corridor suddenly glowed with a lovely light, a light that brought out the beauty of the rosy and ruddy marble with which the walls were lined. He had paused at the threshold of a Cabinet meeting to play his part in the dedication of the world's loftiest office building.

Al Smith took off his black derby and waved it. "Come on, everybody!" he shouted. "Follow me and we'll go around to the elevators that will take us up to the eighty-sixth floor, the observatory floor, and when we get there I'll show you the hills of Westchester, the Narrows, and Newark, anything you like. Come on, let's go!" He was as enthusiastic as any boy over a Christmas toy. As he led the crowd like the gay and laughing Pied Piper of Hamelin leading the children, he spoke of its height, its floor space, the history of the site, the dramas that had been enacted during the raising of the structure and of the fate and perils that had gone into the project.

They went up and up and up and up. All the way to the eighty-sixth floor. When they got there, they found a buffet luncheon awaiting them. "I'd like you to remember you are eating higher up in the air than any human being has ever eaten," said Smith. "There may have been loftier meals on mountain tops or in airplanes, but not in buildings. This is the world's record."

The food paled, however, as the guests walked around the observation roof. Their eyes were met with what to many was probably the most dazzling sight they had ever seen. Keep in mind that in those days few people had ever flown in an airplane. From the top, other skyscrapers in the city were dwarfed. They beheld a vast panorama of shimmering water, tall towers, quiet suburban homes, and busy Manhattan streets. Steamers of leviathan size and tugs that appeared to be little more than rowboats could be seen far up the Hudson and East rivers. Down the bay, beyond the Narrows, and out to sea a ship occasionally came into view or faded in the distance.

Before the gaze of the distinguished guests, the city was spread out for miles in every direction. To the north were seen the apartment houses of the Bronx. To the east and southeast, the green residential sections, the business and factory districts and shoreline of Long Island and Brooklyn, all were clearly visible. Beyond the bay could be seen the hills of Staten Island; and to the west, the smoke of Jersey's industries, with wooded slopes hiding thousands of dwellings. In Manhattan the tall buildings, which from the streets below appeared as monsters of steel and stone, assumed a less awe-inspiring significance when viewed from above. Fifth Avenue and Broadway were little more than skinny black ribbons that had cut their way sharply through masses of colored stone and brick. On the avenues lilliputian vehicles jockeyed for position, halting or moving forward in platoons, often like a military procession. From the top of the building, people looked like little more than ants. Their movements could hardly be detected.

Central Park looked like a football field surrounded by the spectator buildings, that hemmed in its lake and trees. The gleaming new apartment houses along the East River were pierced by the spire of the Chrysler tower.

Few of the guests viewing Manhattan Island and the metropolitan area from its highest pinnacle failed to be awed and impressed by the perspective of the smallness of man and his handiwork as seen from such height. They saw men and motor cars creeping like insects through the streets; they saw elevated trains that looked like caterpillars. "There's Central Park, no bigger than a football gridiron," exclaimed one spectator. Gingerly walking up to the parapets, the guests gazed long and intently through the blue haze of a cloudless day, as Governor Smith had invited them to look, across the boundaries of three states and over the Atlantic.

96

He said, "On a clear day, you can take a look at Yonkers, Patchogue, Long Island, Connecticut, Sandy Hook and Plainfield, New Jersey."

It was noon by this time, and down on Thirty-fourth Street there was a scurry and flurry. A siren shrieked east of Fifth Avenue. A motorcycle policeman whirled across the avenue on East 34th Street. Mounted police came along at full gallop, waving motor cars to one side and warning pedestrians to look out. Then along came a very large black limousine, which drew up at the curb on West 34th Street, the entrance of the Empire State Building closest to Broadway. With some difficulty, a tall man stepped out of the car, and on the arm of a companion, made his way to the doorway. It was Governor Franklin Delano Roosevelt, who had come down from the governor's mansion in Albany for the occasion. As he passed, he waved his arm to the right and left, acknowledging the applause of perhaps several thousand people. With his arrival, the luncheon and the official party, except for the presence of Mayor Walker, was complete. Following a buffet luncheon, the spectators assembled in an enclosure on the east side of the eighty-sixth floor, where the formal meeting was held. "The Star-Spangled Banner" was played by the Hotel McAlpin Orchestra, and the ceremony was broadcast by WEAF and WOR.

Ex-Governor Alfred E. Smith rose to his feet and addressed one assemblage. "The officers and the directors of the Empire State, Inc., welcome you to the opening of the new Empire State Building. I desire to read to you a telegram from the White House, Washington:

HON. ALFRED E. SMITH, NEW YORK. I MOST CORDIALLY CONGRATULATE YOU AND YOUR ASSOCIATES UPON THE COMPLETION OF THE EMPIRE STATE BUILDING AND THE OPENING OF ITS DOORS TO THE SERVICE OF THE PUBLIC. THIS ACHIEVEMENT JUSTIFIES PRIDE OF ACCOMPLISHMENT IN EVERY ONE WHO HAD ANY PART IN ITS CONCEPTION AND CONSTRUCTION AND IT MUST LONG REMAIN ONE OF THE OUTSTANDING GLORIES OF A GREAT CITY. HERBERT HOOVER.

Then Smith said, "I have another telegram that I do not propose to read, but propose to say something about. It comes from aboard the

Alfred E. Smith shows Franklin Delano Roosevelt,
then governor of New York State, the view of the city
from the top of the Empire State Building during
the opening festivities, May 1, 1931. *UPI.*

Augusta, some place between here and Italy, and aboard that steamer is John J. Raskob, and this is a long telegram of congratulation to the workmen and to all the people who had anything to do with the construction of the Empire State Building, and it voices, I am sure, a very deep regret on his part that he cannot be with us today.

"Probably no building in the history of the world has brought about such universal interest in its progress. This is practically a holiday in this section, this midtown section of New York City. Interest in this building is not confined to our state or our country; it is universal. We have read articles about it, we have had pictures of it sent to us from newspapers published practically throughout the civilized world. The Empire State Building stands today as the greatest monument to ingenuity, to skill, to brain power, to muscle power, the tallest thing in the world today produced by the hand of man."

Smith continued: "Before I introduce the various speakers, I want to take this occasion to thank our newspaper friends, and thank them very heartily, for the earnest cooperation that they have given to the decorators, contractors, and everybody identified with Empire State over the one year that it took to erect it. I desire also to thank our moving picture friends for the delightful pictures that have been taken of this building. They can be shown all over the world and help to stimulate the interest I just spoke about. The radio—that's right, too—radio has been carrying voices from the top of the Empire State since the first day that they were able to cart the machines up there. To the staff, the working staff of Empire State, the heads of the different departments, the thanks of the directors in full measure, because they have certainly devoted themselves to the interest of this project. To the city officials who have taken an interest in the progress of the building, and to the contractor, Starrett Brothers and Eken, heartfelt thanks. It is a monument to them that will stand here forever. To the architects, Messrs. Shreve, Lamb and Harmon—it is a matter of regret that Mr. Lamb was compelled to sail for Europe yesterday, but I received a telegram from him this morning in which he said, "One day out and I can still see the building."

(Actually, Lamb was not compelled to sail to Europe. His widow, Mrs. William Lamb of New York City, revealed that "he was very modest regard the building. Very shy. When we went abroad in 1931, he planned the trip so that we would sail on the very day of the party. We sailed on the *Ile de France.* That was during Prohibition, you know, so my husband took a little aluminum cocktail shaker filled with martinis along with us. After the three-mile limit we walked out onto the deck, and he threw the empty shaker overboard and said, 'Isn't this marvelous? Here we are and we don't have to go to the party and listen to all those speeches.' As it turned out the speeches were broadcasted on board ship, so we had to listen to them anyway.")

Smith went on with his speech. "Too much praise cannot be given to the faithful workmen that put this monument in the air. I came over here during the course of its construction and it was the cleanest, finest piece of building construction that probably this country has ever known. We propose to put a tablet down in the main hall and inscribe upon it the names of the master craftsmen who received the awards for being the best in their particular line, so that their children and their children's children, when they come in the Empire State, can be able to point to the tablet with the pride that they will feel in the achievement of their forefathers. You remember the little picture that was in the *Evening Post* depicting Tony and his mother on the roof of an East Side tenement, and the mother put her hand on Tony's head, pointed up to the Empire Building, and said, 'Tony, your old man is building that!' And Tony's old man had a large part in the building of it and the mother had a justified pride and we share it with her. I am for the mother, and I am for Tony and for Tony's old man.

"The first ceremonial today was the cutting of the ribbon across the main entrance on Fifth Avenue. That little ceremony was performed by two of my grandchildren, and we had a reason for it. This building is

being built for generations to come down through the ages, and the two small children with scarcely the proper understanding of just what was going on were there to symbolize for all time to come that this building is to be a monument for generations to come."

Smith then paused and turned to present Governor Roosevelt. He looked at him and said, "This building is named after the Empire State of our Union. And on behalf of the officers and directors of the company, I extend a very hearty welcome to the governor of our state, and thank him very sincerely for taking out of his busy life sufficient time to come here and help us dedicate the building. The state of New York can use this building any time it wants to. The governor can have a meeting up here, and if the session lasts into the warm weather, he can bring the thirty-day bills up on the roof here and we will provide him with lemonade, and he can dispose of the state's business at the highest point on the continent. It gives me great pleasure to introduce our Frank, the governor of New York."

Governor Roosevelt rose to applause and said, "Governor Smith and your associates. This building is not called the Empire State Building just because it has been properly erected for the benefit of all of the people of the state of New York, but I think that its name is most highly fitting because it typifies the service that its principal backer and principal builder has rendered to the state of New York during all these years.

"I am still a little awestruck. I have not got my new sense of proportion back yet. In looking out from this building, I have got an entirely new conception of things in this city of New York. As a simple countryman who has only been down here in New York for twenty-five years, I still think in terms of fields and creeks. And when I looked out north and saw Central Park, it reminded me of the sides of my cow pasture at Hyde Park. And when I looked over the Hudson River and East River, they looked from here just about the size of Wappinger Creek, in Duchess County."

Roosevelt continued. "I think that there are two keynotes today. One is the keynote of vision. It took people like Governor Smith and his associates to vision this building. It is only people with their grasp of the needs of the future, with their grasp of possibilities of modern sciences, who could have conceived the building up of a building like this. And the second great thing that this building stands for is faith, because again the governor and his associates are men who have had the faith to carry their visions into effect. And that faith I am very confident is going to be fully justified in the days to come. This building is needed in the city of New York. It is located at a strategic center. It is needed not only by the city, it is needed by the whole nation.

"So I am very happy as a citizen of New York to congratulate all of you, the owners, the managers, builders, and the workmen who made it possible on completing a task in record time"—a record which in fact stands to this day—"in doing it truly and well, and in once more setting a mark of vision and faith that will hold good for many, many years to come.

"I am very happy to have been able to take part today, on the first of May 1931. Nearly a year ago, I said to Governor Smith, 'When is the building to be opened?' He said, 'On May first.' I said, 'I suppose that means the following October.' He said, 'No, you put it down on your calendar.' I did. And once more he has kept his pledge to his associates and to the people. All I am going to ask him to do is reserve for me an office in this building, so that when I leave Albany, I will have some place to go."

The assembled audience cheered, little realizing at the time that FDR would indeed have some place to go when he left Albany, and for a good long time at that. Mr. Smith then replied to the governor: "About that office, we have a good deal to do today, and we are all busy, but the next day you are in town, I will have you down in the rental department."

Mayor James J. Walker arrived as Governor Roosevelt was finishing his address. Smith, in presenting him, said, "We had some queer experiences in the course of the erection and planning of this building, but I think the most cautious man in the world was the lawyer that advised one of our tenants to have a clause put in the lease that in the event the city took over the building that we would repay them part of the money that they had paid in decorating the premises. Well, I said, I don't know, they may try to take it away from us, but I think we can afford to put that in the lease anyway, because I do not think they will do it right away at least."

He continued. "You have noticed that the mayor has just come in to take part in the ceremony. He has a great part in the ceremony. He has a great pride in the building. It is a great moment in the city. It is intended to stimulate trade, commerce, and continue to make New York the imperial city of the world. I therefore, with great pleasure and great satisfaction present to you our own Jimmy, the mayor of New York."

Mayor Walker then said, "It is but a short time ago that I wondered, even with all the resourcefulness of Al Smith, how a building could get up quite this high and wide. But recent developments have convinced me that after all he had not only an interest in official New York, he had a little sympathy for it, and he thought perhaps there might be a place higher, further removed than any other in the world, where some public official might like to come and hide, so he built this."

The audience laughed and applauded.

"I come very seriously, though, to bring a very sincere word of congratulations and felicitation. Obviously this means much to the city of New York, and the pride that naturally is yours and mine, either with or without responsibility of the development of the city of New York, is great. New York's skyline is perhaps the most discussed public institution throughout the world. Day after day, with visitors of the city, the wonder is what is holding us up, I mean the buildings.

"Yet it remained only for a man with the courage, the vision, the knowledge of the city of New York, of its demands, of its necessities, and of its hopes. We find again transcending all others in accomplishment the most beloved son of this city, as the president of this, the greatest construction organization, or the greatest piece of structure in the city of New York. There was a time not long since, when some of us thought that Al was going as high as it was possible to go, now we know that he has exceeded the speed level or the speed time in building.

"New York's skyline is of great interest throughout the world, yet few people know because they have not had sufficient interest to study the great difficulties and the great activities of the city of New York's subsurface. Even while we meet here today, to celebrate this great accomplishment, there is in some quarters of official New York some little unrest. It is the intention of the city to build a subway, and plans have been made for an extension that would go down Sixth Avenue. Yet we find the subsurface of the city of New York has been so crowded that there may be some doubt about the fulfillment, for right down Sixth Avenue there runs a rock tunnel carrying the high water pressure for this city, and now the alarm, temporary, I hope, is that a subway cannot be laid over that lest it injure the water tunnel. This will be overcome. The water tunnel will be protected; the subway will be built; but it is just a sample of the difficulties of keeping abreast of the growth of this city and meeting the demands of people to live in it and do business, without regard to the intricacy and difficulty of meeting these obligations.

"You are quite right, in the opinion of most of us, Governor, that which has settled in the midtown section will grow. The midtown section will become more important in the opinion of official New York, as witnessed by the purpose of building the new Thirty-eighth Street tube. The same vision and the same determination that business shall carry on in the section that is yours, is ours, and as you anticipate, and as your associates anticipate the necessity for this, the biggest building in this locality, so do we conclude that service and comfort for business poeple must be augmented in this same neighborhood.

"I wish for you and your associates that success which your industry, your intelligence, your endeavor deserves. I wish for the great success of the building, so that we shall receive that three hundred fifty-odd thousand dollars of land tax alone that we will be pleased to get from you every year, plus whatever tax is finally decided upon for the building, but I have this consolation in that, and this satisfaction, that no matter what we tax you, you know that it is worth it.

"You know it is the most beautiful building in the city. You know it will be a city in itself when the day closes. There will be poured into the streets a greater population than there is in many of our upstate cities. Again, you will find yourself presiding over another city smaller than you are in the habit of administering to, but they will have the satisfaction of knowing it will be with that characteristic efficiency and with that desire for their comfort that has followed your every public and private activity.

"My best wishes to you, to the success of the building, with the assurance that so far as the city is concerned, it is only waiting for an opportunity to bring to this locality all the necessary conveniences that the business of the community will demand. It has had a great start with the name Empire State, and coupled with that, it seems most natural, is the name of Alfred E. Smith, which in itself is a guarantee of success and long life."

After Walker spoke, Smith presented the spokesman for the architects, saying: "The architects—well, the building is a good enough ad for them without even talking about it. All they have got to do when they see a prospective customer is to say, 'Take a little walk with me down to the corner of Thirty-fourth Street and Fifth Avenue and give it the once-over.' It gives me great pleasure to introduce to you Mr. R. H. Shreve of Shreve, Lamb and Harmon, a man that watched it grow from the big hole in the ground only a year ago to the magnificent structure that we are all in today. Mr. Shreve."

Shreve humbly said the first credit for the building and its aesthetic qualities should go to his colleague, Mr. Lamb, who had faced the necessity of meeting "the impossible demand for speed in construction." He explained that the design was influenced by functionalism, and estimated that the weight of the building was about 600 million pounds. He computed, however, that the great bulk weighed no more than a 45-foot rock pile that might cover its site. He explained that 220 columns supported the burden of the building, and that the structure was vertical within a variation of $5/8$ inch. The load was distributed so evenly that the weight on any given square inch was no greater than that normally borne by a French heel, he declared.

After mentioning that materials had been brought from all over the world, Shreve described how a rush order from Cleveland was speeded up by transmitting details by telephone. We have had an amazingly happy combination of owner, builder, architect, engineer, and worker, he said.

Colonel Paul Starrett, president of Starrett Brothers and Eken, then spoke for the builders, contrasting the colossal building with the tepees of the Indians and the cabins of the first settlers that had once stood on the same spot. After speaking of the early growth of New York City, he continued: "As the years multiplied, far-seeing builders turned their eyes northward to the end that this favored spot, Thirty-fourth Street and Fifth Avenue, became the center of a city within a city. I was a young man when the stately Waldorf was in the building. When the Astoria became its hyphenated neighbor, I still held a few youthful illusions. I recall occasional visits made to the old Waldorf during the days when John W. Gates and his associates of that decade dropped in for the afternoon cocktail. I remember the arrival of Li Hung-chang, with his colorful entourage, when the Chinese flag was flung from the second balcony. I recall the stately dining room and the early days when a nod from Oscar was equivalent to knighthood. I never pass this corner without thinking of the gigantic transactions which took place here, where waiters received magnificent tips on the stock market, handed out by the big speculators with lavish hand.

"Between then and now, in the tumult of life and in business and of progress, great changes have been wrought. The Indians have passed into oblivion; the cabin dwellers still survive through their fortunate heirs; the Waldorf has rejoined the dust and the Empire State Building, which represents the time between that era and today, lifts its head one thousand two hundred fifty feet above the pavement, upon which a billion or more restless feet have trod since the white man came. Few can tell what the future will bring forth. It is not within my province to say what colossal changes will eventuate or how much higher into the reaches our successors will build. But I do know that among those responsible for this present triumph, this present city, and this present Republic, you will find always plenty of those plain citizens, the very vitals of a nation, who are willing at any time to convert dollars into structures and keep the procession of structures moving."

At the conclusion of the ceremonies, Smith invited the guests to take a walk around the outside to look at Westchester, Nassau, New Jersey. Then, in reply to President Hoover's message, he sent the following telegram:

HONORABLE HERBERT HOOVER
THE WHITE HOUSE
WASHINGTON, D.C.

BY DIRECT WIRE FROM THE HIGHEST TELEGRAPH STATION IN THE WORLD ATOP THE EMPIRE STATE ON BEHALF OF OUR DIRECTORS AS WELL AS MYSELF, WE SINCERELY THANK YOU FOR KIND TELEGRAM OF CONGRATULATIONS UPON THE COMPLETION OF THE LARGEST OFFICE BUILDING IN THE WORLD.

ALFRED E. SMITH

During the afternoon, more than 2,000 invited persons inspected the Empire State Building, from the ground floor to the higher of the two observation towers. Then at night Smith threw another gala, a "sky party" on the eighty-second floor, during which the RKO Theater of the Air was broadcast, climaxing the ceremonies marking the formal opening of the building. A bank of WEAF microphones high above Fifth Avenue picked up the special program, beginning at 10:30 P.M.

Smith spoke about "Old New York," when the tower of Trinity Church, down in lower Manhattan, could be seen from Forty-second Street, and Floyd Gibbons, popular radio star and reporter of the period described the view. Comedians Weber and Fields, entertainer Harry Richmond, and singer Helen Morgan, all took part in the broadcast. The musical feature of the first program broadcast from the tower of the building was the first performance of a special march, "The Empire State," written for the occasion by Milton Schwarzwald, director of the Theater of the Air. Following the broadcast, a buffet supper was served to about 200 guests.

That day, the *New York Times* included an editorial about the building entitled "Building in Excelsis." It read:

Today's ceremonies marking completion of the Empire State Building are only a kind of climax to what has long been going on under the eyes of the people of this city. They have seen the audacious plan formed. They have watched the majestic design of the architect taking form in one upward flight after another toward the clouds, and have almost been ready to cry with Daniel Webster at Bunker Hill Monument, "Let it rise!" The whole has been an extraordinary demonstration of what can be done in the way of gigantic architecture when imagination and technical skill and fine taste and ample means and driving executive ability are placed behind a vast project like the Empire State Building. Its chief architect, Mr. Lamb, has already been awarded the gold medal of the Architectural League and has enjoyed acclaim from his professional fellows. As for the contracting builders and the man who has been at the head of the whole enterprise, all they need to do today is to say to the public in the words of Wren: "If you are hunting for our monument, just look around."

Such a union of beauty and strength in a great building makes of it a valuable possession for the whole community. Men and women, boys and girls who have occasion to gaze daily at the splendid lines and massive structure of the Empire State Building will not easily reconcile themselves to architecture that is cheap or mean or even extravagantly whimsical. All must feel also that the Empire State Building is a monumental proof of hopefulness. Those who planned and erected it and found the funds for it must have been firm in the belief that the future of New York is assured, and that its fundamental interests and activities are certain to go on from year to year conquering and to conquer. Thus, today's celebrations are to be thought of as having a significance which extends far beyond the corner of Fifth Avenue and Thirty-fourth Street, and catches up the whole city, with all its diverse elements, yet with common hopes, into its inspiring sweep.

And so, the world's tallest building, the Empire State Building was now open. Twenty-five percent of the space was rented. Now all that remained was to rent the remaining 75 percent, a goal that would not be attained for well over a decade.

5

The Jewel in the Crown of Manhattan

W e have one of these in Siam!" That was what King Prajadhipok of Siam said to Al Smith when he and Queen Rambhai Barni paid a state visit to this country and gazed at the city from the top in July, just after the grand opening. "Oh," said Al Smith, "one of these?" "Yes," replied the king, "a white elephant."

And that was just about the story when the building opened. Aesthetically it was considered a triumph, but financially, well, time would tell. Vaudeville artists enlivened their routines with sketches on "The Empty State Building," "The 102-Story Blunder," and "Smith's Folly." Other wags in town put in their two cents as well. According to Walter Winchell's column, one said, "I see that every girl in town has a likeness of Hoover on her knees. I wish that someone would look at the bottom of Garbo's feet for a blueprint of the Empire State Building." Another Winchell item described a "guy in a yellow plane who seems to think it will give his friends a thrill to see how close he can come to the Empire State Building without hitting it. He usually tries his experiments late at night, and one of these nights he's going to make a mistake and hit it."

But the design was generally applauded. The New York Architectural League awarded the designers its gold medal. And the *New York Times,* in an editorial on April 23, 1931, said:

Granting the gold medal of the Architectural League to the designers of the Empire State Building will have general endorsement. If the matter had been submitted to a referendum in the city, the decision would almost surely have been the same. To have planned and erected such a gigantic structure with a result that is pleasing to the eye as well as appealing to the imagination is a triumph enough for any architect. It may well be true that the rise and completion of the Empire State Building under the eyes of millions of residents here had the effect of heightening the curiosity and concern that surrounded it.

In January 1932 the New York chapter of the American Institute of Architects also bestowed its medal of honor on Shreve, Lamb and Harmon. Stephen F. Voorhees, president of the New York chapter, in presenting the award, said, "In the monumental design of a great office building they have made a genuine contribution to architecture. The noble simplicity of this outstanding structure makes it an inspiring landmark in our city. All members of the firm have given generously of their time to advance the practice of architecture through service in the chapter and other organizations of like purpose."

Critic Douglas Haskell of *The Nation* was particularly impressed with the chrome-nickel-steel strips that soar to the sky on the façade, and that give the building its mystical luster. His article was entitled "A Temple of Jehu," and it began with a quote: "Time is the what with which some dolls are stuffed." It continued:

When they built the Chrysler Building they put on a lot of shiny work just for fun; but not so when they built the Empire State. On top there is a "mooring mast," to be sure, but that was just the publicity man's addition of sex appeal. The shiny metal below is the important thing, the strips of chrome-nickel steel that shinny up the frame like streaks of Jehu. They were not meant to be just "ornamental"—they mean business. Allow me by explaining those metal strips to illustrate a certain fundamental change in the old art of architecture. We used to think of it as associated with "eternity," by which we mean only permanence; but now architecture has become completely the child of time. The dance is hardly more so.

This is how it went. When they figured the economics of the Empire State Building, they decided on eighty-five floors. Yet considering the carrying charges on land worth $16,000,000, they could not afford to wait for all those floors to be built. Being Americans they then decided to build all eighty-five in the time usually required for thirty; and that's where the vertical metal strips come in, as one of the refinements for the sake of speed.

These vertical strips were fastened at intervals directly to the frame, and what they did was to carry forward the principle of articulation. They served to divide the window from the wall. To one side of any strip there could go up a column of stone, to the other side a stack of windows with aluminum panels between. No longer did the window have to be fitted to the stone, or the stone cut to an accurate arris at the window opening, since the metal strip covered the edge. See what that meant: if the stone gang was held up by delay, the window gang nevertheless could proceed. Again: the stones could come from the quarry ready-cut, since there was no further fitting to be done on the job. In short, there was almost such a thing at the Empire State as a factory assembly of standard units. It would have been complete, I believe, except for a few obstacles such as pernicious labor habits and the Building Code.

The Empire State has sixty-seven elevators, traveling 1,000 feet a minute and timed so that in each bank a car leaves every twenty seconds. This enormous core of swift transportation occupying nearly a third of the "cubage" embodies another story, telling how the building got its shape; time entered once more in the choice of a location, and in the guise of "obsolescence" it will cause the building's death. Time is the important fourth dimension of our new buildings, and it is just as integral as the materials are.

Yet I have chosen just the illustration of the metal strips because they worked over so beautifully into the design. While serving their humble use, they flash wonderfully in the sun; they make the character of the enterprise manifest; in their swift upward streak they tell the story—Organization! Speed! When at the top and bottom and in the lobby the designers tried allegory and decoration, they seemed to be merely fumbling around. This despite the fact that Shreve, Lamb, and Harmon are among our keenest planners of buildings—or because of it.

112

Kenneth R. Murchison, former president of the Society of the Beaux Arts Architects, and designer of the Beaux Arts apartment building and other New York structures, said, "The Empire State is New York's most beautiful skyscraper, also the most impressive, but City Hall is New York's most beautiful building, the Woolworth Building is beautiful but this type of skyscraper is not so much so as the New York Telephone Building or the Empire State." According to Mrs. William F. Lamb, Le Corbusier, the great French architect, admired the building very much. And Frank Lloyd Wright once walked through the lobby full of praise for the fine green marble details. He pointed to them with his cane.

But there were those who questioned the practicality of the building. Many newspapers considered it a milestone, marking the advent of a new era in sky-piercing and the obsolescence of the old-fashioned skyscraper. Papers like the *Brooklyn Eagle, Washington Post* and *Star,* the *Cleveland Plain Dealer,* and the *New York World-Telegram* wondered what the future would bring. The *World-Telegram* said:

What does this colossal building signify? What does it prophesy? Are there to be other buildings still higher and vaster? If so, how high and vast?

Where will the people live who occupy them in daytime? How can rapid-transit lines ever be built fast enough? Will gigantic nearby residential piles arise to house the people from the super-sky-scrapers?

Why was the stupendous structure built? Was it conceived to glorify men, to glorify humankind's passion for bigness?

Or is it but an inevitable expression of the new age of giantism, a step in growth just as a new limb is a step in the growth of a California redwood?

The Flatiron Building, the Woolworth Building, the Empire State—these are the three outstanding landmarks in New York's progress into the skies.

What new landmark will make the Empire State an old landmark?

The *Baltimore Sun* wrote, "It would not be amiss to call a halt on height at this point. It requires only a few structures of comparable capacity in a given locality to create traffic and transportation problems of the first magnitude."

Lewis Mumford, in an article entitled "Notes on American Architecture" which appeared in *The New Republic* in 1931, made a few remarks on the Empire State Building. It was tall, he conceded, and he thought its size gained from its simple, four-square mass. But he had no use for the mooring mast. "Nothing could be stupider and sillier." Since it was unlikely to be used for dirigibles, it remained, he supposed, "in order to reinforce its claim to being the highest building in the world—as if that fact were of the slightest importance."

Architect Buckminster Fuller apparently was not too impressed with the building. He is reported to have suggested that in order to save lives lost during the construction, the building should have been constructed laterally and then raised up into place. The column in Saint Peter's Square in Rome was placed in position in this manner. And in fact, apparently, he proved that it could have been done in that way.

Karl Schriftgiesser said in the *Boston Transcript* that

this monument to New York's passion for the superlative in all things is possibly the end of America's if not the world's Golden Age of building or else only a step in the beginning. Present day architecture is not architecture for the ages, it is architecture for Now. Whether the floor space in Empire State will be absorbed at once is immaterial. The building is there and as one by one the little buildings of the past that still are here and there on Manhattan empty out because of age and inconvenience the huger, new ones fill up. Empire State will find its twenty-five thousand people in due time.

When it has found them, other buildings will take its place. When Louis Sullivan or Frank Lloyd Wright, in earlier days saw steel as the structural basis of the new building, when Cass Gilbert traced the Woolworth Building on his drawing board, such hugeness as Empire State was not conceived. But mankind has caught up with the dreams of the poet builders, and it stands strong, solid, unswaying above Manhattan, tallest arrow in the quiver.

Now it was time for the public to inspect the building. The day after the gala opening, on a Sunday, crowds thronged to the site to view the marble lobby and to experience the most spectacular view in the world. A steady stream of visitors, numbering 5,108, roamed through the corridors and then went up to the observation platform. Down on Fifth Avenue the scene was something like a carnival. On the sidewalks where the old Waldorf once stood were peddlers of carnations, candy, and souvenirs. All were doing a thriving business among the thousands who had come to see the new structure.

At ten o'clock, and even before that hour, the line had already formed. It was a clear, shining day, one of the best for looking down on the city. Comments from the sightseers were varied, but two things seemed to stand out. One, that "Central Park looked like a small pasture dotted with tiny puddles of rainwater," and the other, that the Chrysler Building, until just a few weeks before the tallest building in the world, looked like a toy. Even on the outside the crowds formed, and extra policemen were put on duty to see to it that a jam didn't occur on the sidewalks. Certainly, although prospective tenants were not banging the doors down to get office space, the public was, to see the view. One month later, almost 100,000 persons had paid one dollar a head to go to the top. At that rate, over 1 million paid tourists a year were ultimately to keep the building afloat through the lean years of the Great Depression.

And how did visitors feel about what they saw? Overwhelmed indeed, and they continued to be. However, perhaps one of the most interesting impressions came from Helen Keller, who, through blind eyes, "saw" New York from the top in January of 1932. She wrote in the *New York Times* on January 17 about her experience:

What did I think "of the sight" when I was on the top of the Empire State Building? Frankly, I was so entranced "seeing" that I did not think about the sight. If there was a subconscious thought of it, it was in the nature of gratitude to God for having given the blind seeing minds. As I now recall the View I had from the Empire Tower, I am convinced that until we have looked into darkness, we cannot know what a divine thing vision is.

Perhaps I beheld a brighter prospect than my companions with two good eyes. Anyway, a blind friend gave me the best description I had of the Empire Building until I saw it myself.

Do I hear you reply, "I suppose to you it is a reasonable thesis that the universe is all a dream, and that the blind only are awake?" Yes—no doubt I shall be left at the Last Day on the other bank defending the incredible prodigies of the unseen world, and, more incredible still, the strange grass and skies the blind behold are greener grass and bluer skies than ordinary eyes see.

I will concede that my guides saw a thousand things that escaped me from the top of the Empire State Building, but I am not envious. For imagination creates distances and horizons that reach to the end of the world. It is as easy for the mind to think in stars as in cobble-stones. Sightless Milton dreamed visions no one else could see. Radiant with an inward light, he sends forth rays by which mankind beholds the realms of Paradise.

But what of the Empire State Building? It was a thrilling experience to be whizzed in a "lift" a quarter of a mile heavenward, and to see New York spread out like a marvelous tapestry beneath us. There was the Hudson!—more like the flash of a sword-blade than a noble river. The little island of Manhattan, set like a jewel in its nest of rainbow waters, stared up into my face, and the solar system circled about my head!

Why, I thought, the sun and the stars are suburbs of New York and I never knew it! I had a sort of wild desire to invest in a bit of real estate on one of the planets. All sense of depression and hard times vanished; I felt like being frivolous with the stars. But that was only for a moment. I am too static to feel quite natural in a Star View cottage on the Milky Way, which must be something of a merry-go-round even on quiet days.

I was pleasantly surprised to find the Empire State Building so poetical. From every one except my blind friend I had received an impression of sordid materialism—the piling up of one steel honeycomb upon another with no real purpose but to satisfy the American craving for the superlative in everything. A Frenchman has said: In his exalted moments the American fancies himself a demigod, nay a god; for only gods never tire of the prodigious. The highest, the largest, the most costly is the breath of his vanity.

Well, I see in the Empire State Building something else—passionate skill, arduous and fearless idealism. The tallest building is a victory of imagination. Instead of crouching close to earth like a beast, the spirit of man soars to higher regions, and from this new point of vantage he looks upon the impossible with fortified courage and dreams yet more magnificent enterprises.

What did I "see and hear" from the Empire tower? As I stood there 'twixt earth and sky I saw a romantic structure wrought by human brains and hands that is to the burning eye of the sun a rival luminary. I saw it stand erect and serene in the midst of storm and the tumult of elemental commotion. I heard the hammer of Thor ring when the shaft began to rise upward. I saw the unconquerable steel, the flash of testing flames, the swordlike rivets. I heard the steam drills in pandemonium, I saw countless skilled workers welding together that mighty symmetry. I looked upon the marvel of frail yet indomitable hands that lifted the tower to its dominating height.

Let cynics and supersensitive souls say what they will about American materialism and machine civilization. Beneath the surface are poetry, mysticism and inspiration that the Empire State Building somehow symbolizes. In that giant shaft I see a groping toward beauty and spiritual vision. I am one of those who see and yet believe.

Another gentleman wasn't quite as enthusiastic. In fact he was terrified. He was a famous aviator who brought with him a stationary height phobia. While he was utterly unafraid when flying, he found stationary heights unendurable. Although the walls surrounding the outer terraces of the observatory were 3 feet 7 inches high, the aviator, who had flown thousands of miles in every conceivable height without a qualm, stayed inside the glass-enclosed section of the observatory. He only stuck his head out of the window to bellow to his wife to "come away from the wall."

His wife, who had an equally deep-seated fear of flying, was so free and unafraid she would have liked to climb all the way to the very top of the tower.

One of the most interesting reactions was that of Kata Ragoso, king of Morovo in the Solomon Islands. He arrived at the tower one afternoon, a giant chieftain with a great shock of kinky hair forming a wide halo around his head. He wore a long singlet instead of pants, and his feet and legs were bare. The club with which his cannibal father had killed forty people swung at his belt, but only as a reminder to him of the distance he had traveled from cannibalism to Christianity, for he himself was a Seventh-Day Adventist missionary. Quite indifferent to the interest and curiosity of the hundreds of people who followed him from the entrance to the terrace, the king abandoned himself, like a child, to the pure joy of his experience. He ran around and around, clapping his hands, wrinkling his nose, continually shouting: "Oh, that's great! Oh, that's great!"

A young Mexican girl, driving through New York from her home in

Texas, was glib enough about New York sights until she got to the top of the building. As she stepped out onto the 102nd-floor terrace and gazed over the city, she trembled with emotion and cried. Finally she said she would "rather be in Texas. Everything here is so big it frightens me."

And what did the "sky boys" who had built the building think about "their" building? An interpretation of their point of view was offered by Earl Sparling in the *New York World-Telegram*. He couched his story in terms of an imaginary monology from one sky boy to another, in the mood of emptiness and depression that comes when the big job is done, and life holds nothing but a vague thought of the next tower to be built. Even the weather is all wrong. It appears to this "morning after" pessimist that fog and rain will always conspire to hide the greatest trophy of his toil.

Up here, 102 stories high, a quarter of a mile above the sidewalks, you really can't see very much.

That, Joe, is the joke of it.

Remember, we talked about that months ago, when you and the rest of the gang were topping out on the 86th floor.

You said, "We'll build them higher than this some day." And you added, "But what's the use? When you get up this high, all you get is rain and fog."

It seems a long time now, that day when the forge fire glowed right in the middle of the eighty-sixth floor and the tower was still just a mass of steel girding against a rainy sky. It's different now.

Everything is warm and cozy up here now. Men in spats are standing in line at $1 per, to look out over the bulwarks and young mothers are bringing their children up, and over on one of the soft bamboo settees two young tourist newly-weds are making love shamelessly.

Seeing those mothers with their children reminded me of something, Joe. You didn't say much that day, but I sort of got the idea. It wasn't what you said but the way old Freddy hunched over the wheel-barrow fire when I mentioned the lives lost.

I got to thinking to-day and I tried to pick out the shaft that carpenter went down. I couldn't find it.

All the shafts look alike now, and the elevator operators are drest up in swell uniforms and when the elevators go up and down the men in the spats complain that their ears buzz.

It doesn't seem possible that only a few months ago there was a fire in the wheel-barrow right where the souvenir counter stands now.

Boy, it was cold that day, and thanks for that drink. Is the old Scotchman still at it? He better cut it out. You can't build this kind of thing with whisky. He'll probably get it on the Metropolitan job if he doesn't cut it out.

Sure. I got it pretty straight today. They're figuring on 110 stories, and 110 stories would be a long way to fall, even drunk.

A series of light spring fogs interfered with visibility for a few days after the opening, and Sparling reflects this in his story.

I found myself leaning over the bulwarks, just now, alongside of a fat guy with an accent.

He said, "I was in the Woolworth Building. It was better. You was able to see something. It was down below the clouds and you could see something."

As a matter of fact he was about right. Not being able to see very much, the customers have started a habit of scratching their initials in the steel walls up in the tower-room. That ought to give you a laugh, Joe. You birds risk your lives building a building like this so that birds like that can come up and scratch their initials against the sky.

Now the time had come for fun. Al Smith was determined to make the Empire State Building the symbol of New York, the main attraction superseding everything, including the Statue of Liberty herself. Everybody who came to visit the city on official auspices was treated to the view from the top, and publicity stunts and hilarious escapades were recounted almost daily in the newspapers. The parade of celebrated visitors began with Prince Takamatsui, brother of the emperor of Japan, and his wife, the Princess Kikooko. Following them came Max Schmeling, the German ex-heavyweight champion of the world. Dr. Dafoe, who had delivered the Dionne quintuplets, was next. Then George Bernard Shaw, who acted a great deal like the Americans he often called "boobs." He nearly wriggled out of the window of his car in his efforts to get a good look at the building, beginning to crane his neck as soon as the spire glittered at him from up Fifth Avenue. Since those days the list has included hundreds of heads of state, famous stars of the motion picture and TV worlds, some 365 celebrities a year, about one a day. Sir Winston Churchill, Queen Elizabeth

II and Prince Philip, Queen Mother Elizabeth of England, Princess Margaret and Lord Snowdon, Nikita Khrushchev, Fidel Castro, King Constantine of Greece, General Zhukov of Bulgaria, the Shah of Iran, and on and on and on. Skating troupes, Follies girls, circus acrobats, bathing beauties, Boy Scouts—and back in 1932 the Polish Olympic ski team.

On their visit to New York, the team decided on a February day to discard their skis to gain a foothold on the metallic steps of Manhattan's loftiest peak. Five members of the team, who were also expert mountain climbers, conquered the heights of the greatest skyscraper on foot. When the team reached the 86th floor they immediately continued on up to the 102nd—and there, when they met the Czechoslovakian skiing team, which had entered the building unannounced a half hour before, they met a challenge. Czechoslovakia didn't want to be outdone by Poland, so George Janecek, Czechoslovakian consulate attaché, offered his country's Olympic team in competition, reminding inquirers that, since its members had fared better in the fifty-kilometer ski race at Lake Placid than had some of the Polish team, they might also win in a "mountain climbing" contest.

The guardians of the Empire State Building, however, were not agreeable with the proposal to use the staircase for international sports competitions. Some of the attendants seemed provoked with the idea of strangers romping all over the building, so competition was called off and the laurels left with Poland.

Through the years many have made the climb. In 1939 the Yale track team climbed to the top en masse, and then in 1941 two Bronx youngsters started out and hoofed it all the way to the top. They were rewarded with tea, crumpets, and an introduction to Al Smith. There was also a Scottish lad who arrived in New York shortly after the building was finished, his one ambition to see the world from its great height. One day he pooled his last six cents with another lad who had a nickel. This got them from Brooklyn to New York on the subway. Neither knew how they would get to the top or how they would get home, but they took their

Winston Churchill and Alfred E. Smith
at the 86th-floor observatory.

chance. Luck was with them, as they managed to evade all the first-floor guards, find the stairway, and climb to the top without a mishap.

In June of 1932 the first marriage performed on the tower took place at midnight, when Miss Doris Averell of Springfield, Massachusetts, became the bride of Mr. William Holmes of Weehawken, New Jersey. They met when Holmes, who was then a director of physical education at the Hoboken, New Jersey, YMCA, was a student at Springfield College. Visitors to the tower crowded around the couple and their wedding guests, a party of thirteen, to see the ceremony performed.

And then on the night of August 11, 1932, one of the more elaborate publicity stunts took place. The famous magician Dunninger had offered $10,000 to anyone who could produce a real spirit as well as he produced fake ones. A medium, Mrs. Werner, took him up on the deal, and a seance was staged in a darkened room near the top of the building, on one of the tower floors. According to reports, Mrs. Werner, who was sitting before the gathered assemblage, suddenly grew very tense. Her husband, who was with her, called for the lights to be turned out, leaving but a dim red glow. Her tenseness and rigidity growing more and more intense, she sat there for a long period of time, making awkward gestures and emitting sighing sounds. Then she turned her face toward heaven. "She's going to get a message from Thomas Edison!" Mr. Werner muttered.

The lights were thrown on again, and the medium rose and clutched Dunninger's hand. Then she began to mutter in broken English with a smattering of German.

"Is this Mr. Edison?" asked Dunninger.

"Yes," said Edison through his present control, "I am here."

Dunninger then asked, "Do you remember our last conversation?"

"Yes," was the reply.

"Can you tell me anything about it?" queried Dunninger.

"I'm sorry," came the answer in the German accent of Mrs. Werner.

The questions and variants of them were repeated a dozen times, but the control couldn't seem to recall any of the words or even any of the incidents involved in Mr. Dunninger's last meeting with the inventor. Finally, Mrs. Werner wobbled, grew limp, and was assisted into a chair to recover from her trance.

Mr. Dunninger got up and said, "I think you will agree, my friends, that nothing authentic was presented here this evening. And now, so as not to disappoint you, I will perform a couple of my spirit tricks for you."

A few of the impartial jury remained for the tricks, but most ran up to the eighty-sixth-floor observatory, which is even nearer to heaven, to refresh their own spirits with the view of Manhattan.

The following year Brian Roach, a broncobuster with the rodeo then performing at Madison Square Garden, was invited to visit the Empire State and to bring his horse with him. Horse and rider rode into the lobby, entered an elevator, and ascended to the top. Later in the year K. L. Morehouse, who had invented a tiny car that cost $9,000 and traveled at 130 miles per hour, was also invited to visit. He drove his little car, which contained five diamond-studded bearings, into the building and also went to the top.

Then, in 1934, a little bit of spice was added to the lore of the building, as the observation tower became the place for a lover's tryst that was to become a sensational scandal. It all came out at the trial. Tillie Losch, the Hungarian dancer, was being sued for divorce by her husband, Edward F. W. James. Prince Serge Obolensky was named correspondent. Apparently, James had had his wife tailed by private detectives, and one night after a performance by Miss Losch on Broadway, she, the Prince, Lady Cavendish (the former Adele Astaire), and an unnamed man left the theater and went to the roof of the building. James accused the pair of having a romantic moonlit tryst on New York's loftiest rooftop.

However, all was not frivolous. In March of 1932, when the Lindbergh baby was kidnaped and all the world sat waiting for news, the Empire

State was pressed into service. Signals had been arranged in Hopewell, New Jersey. If the baby was returned by the kidnapers, the historic fire gong in the town would break its silence of twenty years. At the same time, word would be phoned to the Empire State, where floodlights would illuminate the tower and flash on and off for five minutes every half hour, signaling the return. The lights, visible for fifty miles, were, tragically, never called into service.

Then, in November of 1932, a beacon was again pressed into service—this time, to keep the public informed of the results of the presidential election. A beam of light which scanned up and down to the north indicated a Roosevelt lead, while a steady beam to the north indicated a Roosevelt win. The opposite was the case for Hoover.

Ultimately the steady beam to the north indicated Roosevelt's victory.

On a night in 1933, the first tragedy struck the building. It was cold and blustery, and the wind screamed around the observation tower. There were only four or five people atop; it was early, and besides, being the thirteenth of the month, few superstitious souls would venture out. The guard was more than pleased when a pretty young girl came up to him and asked him questions. He leaned against the wind and pointed out to the majestic loop of lights, far up on the Hudson, strung along the George Washington Bridge. Looking out to sea, miles beneath them, was the single beacon atop Miss Liberty's arm. The girl nodded absentmindedly at his story, but while the guard and the other customers were looking down into the brilliantly lit heart of Manhattan, the pretty brunette walked perilously onto the ledge, 1,050 feet and five city blocks up in the air. She poised there for a moment, a lone girl teetering on the threshold of death, but by the time the tower guard casually turned back, Irma Eberhardt had sailed out into space like some huge bird and hurtled to her death. Perhaps the howling winds had lured her into leaping with such courage, because had she not sailed into the winds horizontally for 48 feet, she would not have cleared the ledge two stories below her.

Meanwhile, at the Charles Street Police Station, a pale-faced young man was breathlessly pleading with police. He had taken his girl to dinner, left briefly, and came back to find her gone. Finally, he was paged. She had called and said, "I am breaking my promise. I am going to commit suicide." "Do something," the young man demanded of the police. The police phone rang. An unidentified body had just landed on the Empire State marquee, shattering the roof and breaking the lights. A YWCA card, 83 cents and a lipstick were found. The name—oh yes, Irma Eberhardt.

All that night Irma's friend sat there pouring out his grief and his love. He had known her for over a year. The night before, in his parents' home in Flushing, she had quarreled with him because he played basketball nights and neglected her. He had quarreled with her because she dated other men. Finally she said disconsolately, "There's nothing for me to live for. I am going to commit suicide." He had worried, so much so that he hurried to her side as soon as he finished work the next day and pleaded with her to dine with him, to forgive him, and never again to mention the word "suicide." She promised.

At the building, the managers were greatly upset. Appreciating the risk, they had guarded carefully against "leapers." Ticket men refused admission to wild-eyed customers. Guards had been on the "qui vive," and to that point had had only one leaper, a man who failed to clear the obstructing eighty-fourth-story ledge and suffered only broken bones. Irma's was the first fatal leap from man's highest pinnacle.

By 1947 twelve people had leaped to their deaths. The thirteenth occurred when a man hurled himself from the eighty-sixth-floor outdoor observation platform. By some peculiar freak of gusty winds, he didn't land on one of the setbacks that occur between the eighty-sixth floor and the street. Immediately after that, a wire barrier was constructed, on top of a permanent shoulder-high stone wall twice the height of the old one. A reasonably agile man could get over this, but he would incur cuts; apparently, a man bent upon self-destruction is reluctant to cut himself in

(Overleaf) King Kong atop the tower in his doomed struggle against civilization.

the process. In May of 1947 Miss Evelyn McHale, a despondent book-keeper, jumped the entire eighty-six floors, landing on the roof of a sedan parked on the north side of Thirty-third Street. Then, in 1963, sixteen years later, George Alex Frost, a man who had been institutionalized three times, brought the number of jumpers to fifteen. Since then, there has been only one other leap, in 1970, when a young man jumped to his death from the sixty-seventh floor.

In 1933 Hollywood used the Empire State Building in the climax of what has become one of filmdom's golden classics. *King Kong*, starring Fay Wray, and adapted from an imaginative story by the late Edgar Wallace and Miriam C. Cooper, showed the central character, a pre-historic ape over fifty feet tall, making a defiant stand, in the name of love, against a squadron of army combat planes, which are trying to shoot him off the top of the building. In many ways the story line is quite similar to that of *The Hunchback of Notre Dame*. Kong and the Empire State are to New York what the Hunchback and Notre Dame are to the City of Light.

Kong was in production for two years, and represents one of the most ambitious undertakings in composite motion picture photography ever attempted. Due to the exacting detail necessary to maintain the scene in proper perspective, and the seemingly insurmountable technical difficulties involved, production work netted an average of only five completed feet a day, about one-fiftieth of the daily footage of the usual Hollywood product at that time.

King Kong, often called the only monster we can truly believe in, has assured that, come holocaust or demolition, the Empire State Building will remain immortal.

As the thirties wore on and the country sank deeper and deeper into the Great Depression, the fun continued, although the rentals did not increase. A little more than half the building was occupied. Indeed, it was the income from tourists going to the top that helped keep the building afloat financially.

When World War II plunged the earth into military combat, the Empire State was pressed into service. Bond drives and war efforts of endless variety received shots in the arm by being kicked off on the observation platform.

Al Smith died in 1944, and when he did much of the fun associated with the building died with him. His daughter, Mrs. Emily Smith Warner, said. "The Empire State Building was the greatest attraction in the world, along with my father, who was almost the second greatest attraction."

A year later the days of the depression and of World War II came to an end, and the Empire State Building entered an era of peace and prosperity. Office occupancy in the city rose to 98 percent, and the long corridors up there high above the city, dark for so many years, were bathed in light and bustling with activity.

The Day the Airplane Hit the Empire State

The morning of July 28, 1945, was an overcast one in the city. A light drizzle fell gently through the fog. The temperature was a mild 67 degrees Fahrenheit, and the wind, just a breeze, was from the northeast at 5 miles per hour. The cloud ceiling was 1,700 feet and visibility was $2\frac{1}{2}$ miles. Gray mists enveloped the observation tower of the Empire State Building. When viewed from the streets below, it stood like a giant shroud, with the observation tower barely visible.

Meanwhile, up in Bedford, Massachusetts, twenty-seven-year-old Lieutenant Colonel William F. Smith of Watertown, Massachusetts, deputy commander of the 457th Bomber Group, taxied his United States Army Air Force B-25 Mitchell bomber down the runway and took off on the final leg of a cross-country mission that had originated in Sioux Falls, South Dakota. The war in Europe had been over since May 7, and the pilot, a decorated veteran of thirty-four bombing missions in Europe, was piling up cross-country experience as he awaited redeployment to the Pacific. The war against Japan would not be over until August 14. Accompanied by his crew member, Staff Sergeant Christopher S. Domitro-

vitch of Granite City, Illinois, and a navy machinist's mate who had hitched a ride home to Brooklyn to see his parents, he was on his way to Newark Airport in New Jersey, just a few miles from the heart of Manhattan. As his plane approached the metropolitan area, he radioed the control tower at La Guardia field, named after Fiorello H. La Guardia, who was then mayor, informing them that he was fifteen miles to the south. At the same time, he requested information about the Newark weather. Since the bomber's location at the time was close to Newark, the chief operator, Victor Barden, suggested that the colonel call Newark.

Within two minutes, however, the plane appeared directly southeast of La Guardia Field, and Barden, thinking that it was about to land, gave the necessary information about which runway to use, as well as the wind velocity and direction. However, Smith radioed back that he wished to go on to Newark as originally planned. The tower then made contact with Airways Traffic Control, which reported that there was a 600-foot ceiling at Newark and suggested that the plane be held at La Guardia. Then the tower communicated with Army Advisory Flight Control for authorization to bring the bomber into La Guardia, for since this was an army aircraft, instructions had to be issued from the AAFC. The army told the tower that the Newark weather report was erroneous, that actually there was a 1,000-foot ceiling and $2\frac{1}{4}$ miles visibility at Newark. The tower at La Guardia then cleared him to Newark and stated that they were "unable to see the top of the Empire State Building," but that he would clear with 3 miles forward visibility. They further stated that if he was unable to obtain 3 miles forward visibility, he was to return to La Guardia. Contact clearance was definite.

Traveling at 200 miles per hour, the twelve-ton aircraft then headed for Newark Airport. When the plane crossed the East River over Manhattan, it was just north of Forty-second Street, apparently headed southwest. It was flying, not at an altitude of 2,000 feet, the limit then prescribed by the Civil Aeronautics Board for over-city flights, but rather at about 1,000 feet. Spectators in the Grand Central Station heard the roar, and looking up, feared the plane would hit the towering Grand Central Office Building astride Park Avenue. A witness said the plane was no higher than the twenty-second floor at this point. Then it banked and missed the building. In banking to avoid the Grand Central Building, it next just narrowly missed the 500 Fifth Avenue building. Thousands of office workers and Saturday morning strollers and shoppers watched in horror as they saw the big twin-motored Mitchell trying desperately to fight its way out of the maze of midtown office buildings. Witnesses disagreed, but most of them did agree that the pilot was having engine or rudder difficulty, and that he had not blundered carelessly into the stone traps formed by the high buildings of midtown Manhattan that suddenly surrounded him. Confused and surrounded by towers on all sides, Smith seemed to be in the clouds about half the time it took him to cross Manhattan diagonally from the East River. One Army Air Force man who witnessed the catastrophe said that he was certain that the plane "weaved," and another said "it was definitely having rudder trouble."

As the roar of the engines echoed throughout the midtown area, thousands of persons looked up or out of their windows. Many said the plane wobbled before the pilot made a last-ditch effort to evade the world's largest building, as it suddenly appeared before him out of the mist. Another said the pilot was descending from a cloud as he crossed Forty-second Street heading directly for the Empire State Building.

Stan Lomax, the radio sports announcer, was driving to work when he heard the motors and looked up. He and many others automatically shouted to the pilot of the plane to "Climb!" but in a second the aircraft crashed straight on into the side of the building. Lomax said he saw the left wing catapult over toward Madison Avenue. Another eyewitness, Miss Delia M. Delap, an employee of Lord & Taylor, was at home in the Hotel Gregorian. She was on the roof, where she had gone to "look at the weather." "Suddenly the plane roared in and I couldn't see it, but I heard an awful crash," she said. "I ran inside for a moment, then came back out, and the building was all in flames. They covered the top of the building in about two seconds." Allen Ullman, an artist, was standing at Fifth Avenue and Thirty-fifth Street when he saw the plane heading for the building. It seemed to be in no difficulty, he said, "but at the last minute tried to maneuver away to safety."

Mrs. Marion B. Jordan and Miss Alice E. Stover were walking along Madison Avenue between Thirty-ninth and Fortieth Streets when they heard the crash. They turned around to see debris sailing down the side of the Empire State Building. Lieutenant Frank Covey of the Army Air Force saw the crash from his room in the Biltmore Hotel. "I couldn't know if it was out of control," he said. "There were flames from the top of the building down to the twentieth floor. Pieces started shattering down. I watched the flames rip through the building."

From his fifteenth-floor windows on West Forty-second Street, Dr. Bernard Rosenberg, a dentist, after hearing the engines of the plane, and sensing that it was too low, looked out to see the flash of the explosion against the building. A patient said they could see flaming debris floating down the sides of the damaged building.

Employees of the communications division of the Raytheon Manufacturing Company, on the fifty-third and fifty-fourth floors of the Lincoln Building on East Forty-second Street, heard the plane apparently buzzing the midtown area, and those who were facing the windows looking south were horrified when they saw the upper part of the big skyscraper burst into flame, with fiery debris floating down through the mist. D. K. de Neuf, the assistant manager, immediately called La Guardia Field and reported the crash, but the operator at the field was so incredulous that he had to assure him it was not a hoax. De Neuf also notified the control tower at Mitchell Field and the Eastern Sea Frontier headquarters. In all three cases he gave them their first report of the disaster.

Up on the eleventh floor of the New York Times Building on Times Square, a typewriter mechanic, Alfred Spalthoff, was sitting in the cafeteria munching a tuna fish sandwich. He saw the plane traveling on a downward slope at about 200 miles per hour. It was just emerging from the fog and heading straight for the Empire State Building. "When it hit there was a big explosion that seemed to come from four or five of the floors at once. On the Thirty-fourth Street side, and also on the western side of the building, it seemed to go up in flames, blazing fiercely. I watched for parts of the plane to drop but saw none of them."

Yes, it had happened. What people had feared for many years, particularly since the war. A low-flying airplane, fog bound, had crashed directly into the world's tallest building at exactly 9:52 A.M. that Saturday.

Inside the building at that dreadful moment, many people reported their reactions. After the impact, the building moved twice and then settled. One man, who had recently returned from China after twenty-seven years, told of his sensations. He said the impact was precisely that of an earthquake, to which he was no stranger. He said he felt the double movement or shifting of the building first, and then the settling. "It was the settling, not the shaking I was afraid of," he declared. "When I felt the building move once, and move again, and then settle, I said to myself, 'This is it.' I knew from previous experience that a shaking meant only a slight tremor. It was the movement and the settling that I feared. This could be nothing else but an earthquake. My mind at the moment could not tell that I was in New York and not in China, that I was in the Empire State Building. The convulsion after the settling failed to materialize, and I was brought back to my senses. It was not until I had made my way down to the lobby that I found out what happened."

Marwin K. Hart of the National Economics Council was in his office on the seventy-fifth floor of the building. The office and those near by were all but empty. A girl was in an office two rooms away. After being brought to safety, she said, "The building very definitely rocked. It was confusing for a minute. I thought it might fall apart. We have one window on the west side and the windows there were all gone. I looked out to see, leaning out our window. We could see what was left of the plane. The forecart stuck there. The rest of it fell on the south side of the building. Another building to the south, across Thirty-third Street, was on fire. Something had come through and struck it." According to Hart, he rushed out into the hall and found it filled with smoke and the elevator shafts burning. He went to the fire shafts, and they too were filled with smoke. He then went back and got the girl in the other office, and they decided to remain where they were, which they did for an hour, until firemen finally reached them and escorted them out.

With what can only be described as a terrific crash, the United States Army Air Force bomber smashed violently, with terrifying impact, into the building at approximately the seventy-ninth floor level, at a point slightly west of the vertical center of the north side, some 900 feet above Thirty-fourth Street. The plane did not rebound or ricochet from the building, but with its wings sheared off, plunged into the skyscraper, tearing a hole 18 feet wide by 20 feet high in the façade. Brilliant orange flames shot up as high as the observatory on the eighty-sixth floor of the building, 1,050 feet above the street, as the gasoline tanks of the plane exploded. For a moment, spectators in the street below saw the mist-shrouded tower clearly illuminated by the glare. Then it disappeared again in gray murk and the smoke of the burning plane.

The greater portion of the aircraft continued on into the interior of the seventy-eighth and seventy-ninth floors, with a portion continuing a distance of some eighty feet across the waist of the building. One motor hurled down a corridor, clear across the seventy-ninth floor and out the south wall of the building, plummeting down the West Thirty-third Street façade and crashing through the roof of a twelve-story building on the opposite side of West Thirty-third Street. It set fire to and demolished the penthouse of Henry Hering, the sculptor, with resulting damage estimated at $75,000.

The plane's gasoline tanks were ruptured, and gasoline was sprayed over the westerly halves of the seventy-eighth and seventy-ninth floors. The amount of gasoline that was in the 975-gallon-capacity tanks of the plane at the time of the crash is said to have been about 800 gallons. Fire followed the crash as the gasoline was ignited with an explosive force, and the westerly half of the two floors became almost a total mass of fire. Gasoline also descended one elevator shaft, causing a shaft fire all the way down to the basement level.

When the crash occurred, one motor smashed through the base of the shaft of one of the observatory elevators on the seventy-eighth floor. It continued across the elevator hallway, through an eight-inch-thick brick wall enclosing the vent shaft of the fire tower, skipped across the shaftway to the opposite eight-inch brick wall and came to rest in the passageway to the stairs of the fire tower, blocking this passageway completely. A large portion of the motor was torn loose from it, and together with a heavy cast-iron elevator weight carried along from the base of the elevator shaft, plunged down the vent shaftway of the fire tower to the fifty-fourth floor.

On its devastating journey, the plane hit an I-beam in an elevator shaft, causing two elevators to make a sheer drop from the eighteenth to the sub-basement. Miraculously the woman operator of one of the elevators, although seriously injured, survived the fall; the car was practically demolished. All ten elevators in the observation section of the building were put out of commission. At the time of the crash, five elevators were operating between the sixty-sixth and eightieth floors. Some twenty-five passengers were injured when the elevators fell. However, because of the hour and the day, most of the elevators were without passengers. It took fully an hour for some of the women operators to be rescued. Badly burned, they were carried out of the cars. One woman, her face blackened, was still able to walk with support. Still another was locked tight in her compartment, and firemen had to cut a hole in the elevator to rescue her.

The tail section of the plane and other debris fell from the seventy-ninth floor and landed, miraculously, on a setback of the building on the Thirty-fourth Street side landing of the sixth-floor level. It knocked a hole 5 feet in diameter in the reinforced concrete roof, the setback, and the hanging ceiling below, but did not carry through into the building. A private office on the fifth floor, under where the tail assembly struck, was unoccupied. A very small part of the plane fell into West Thirty-fourth Street, but caused no damage.

The seventy-ninth floor of the building was occupied by the War Relief Service of the National Catholic Welfare Conference. Because it was a Saturday, the office was not operating with full staff; however, when the crash came and the cascading torrents of flaming gasoline poured through the seventy-eighth and seventy-ninth floors, everything that was combustible was aflame. Burning fuel ran down stairwells into hallways, while choking fumes and smoke filled the floor. Between fifteen and twenty persons, most of them women clerical workers, were at the office. Eleven of them perished in the inferno. Some managed to run in terror for the doors; at least four safely reached the haven of the fireproof stairwell, but several were overtaken by the flames as they ran, and were burned to death. Three of them who had sought shelter in a separate office at the south side of the building were followed and killed there by the flames.

Paul Dearing, a thirty-seven-year-old volunteer publicity man for the service, saw the flames approaching his desk near the west wall of the building and jumped from a nearby window. He struck a ledge outside the seventy-second floor and was killed. The bodies of Lieutenant Colonel Smith, his crewman, and the navy hitchhiker were burned beyond recognition.

Fortunately, the seventy-eighth floor of the building was unoccupied, was being used for the storage of various building supplies, which helped to keep the death toll down. However, one man, a building employee, was trapped and burned to death there.

Meanwhile, down at street level, indescribable confusion reigned as doctors, nurses, policemen, firemen, newspaper reporters, and servicemen went about their grim tasks. Office workers came streaming out of the elevators that were in operation, but many, cut off, used the stairs to escape the smoke and flames on the upper stories. Seventy, eighty stories, they made their descent, weary but happy to be alive.

Up on the glass-enclosed observation tower on the eighty-sixth floor level, some fifty or sixty men, women, and children were enjoying the view. Frank W. Powell, the tower manager, said that immediately after the crash flames shot up the elevator shafts, followed by a terrific cloud of dust and debris, while metal fragments of the plane landed on the open balcony outside. However, even at that terrible moment the canned music that was wired into the observatory continued to play the lilting sounds of a waltz, reassuring the spectators. There was no panic, but within a few minutes the heat and choking fumes from the fire below made the observatory uncomfortable. The glass doors that lead to the open balcony had been locked to prevent people from wandering out into the fog and slight drizzle that was falling. In the confusion, the keys couldn't be located and so three guards broke the doors open and let in the fresh air. Although some of the spectators rushed for the elevators on the eighty-sixth floor, most followed Powell down to the eightieth-floor elevators and then got to the streets by stairs or elevator.

In the meantime, downtown at City Hall, Mayor Fiorello H. La Guardia was just getting out of his radio-equipped limousine when the fourth alarm sounded. La Guardia, whose appearance at fires in the city were and continue to be legendary, recognized the number of the alarm as that at Fifth Avenue and Thirty-fourth Street. He instructed his driver: "That could be very bad. I'd better go up on that." And so, he sped to the scene. The mayor took the elevator to the sixtieth floor and then walked up to the scene of the disaster. Making his way up, he was soaked from the water cascading down from the fire hoses. When he reached the seventy-ninth floor, he found the "fiery furnace" still raging there, but he remained until after the flames had been put out. After the fire was out, the mayor came down and conferred with John McKenzie, city commissioner of Marine and Aviation, who gave him the details. The animated mayor, the Little Flower, as he was affectionately called, gestured violently with his fist and shouted, "I told them not to fly over the city!"

All things considered, if it had to happen, it happened at the right time, although fourteen people did perish in the calamity. Since it was Saturday, most offices were closed, and the streets below were not jammed with people. The staff of the National Broadcasting Company's TV laboratory on the eighty-fifth floor had not yet arrived to begin the day's work, and the intervening floors between that point and the seventy-ninth were unoccupied. Also, the fact that the bomber hit the building squarely in the middle reduced fatalities. The damage was estimated at $1 million dollars, the building was repaired, and remains today one of the most solidly constructed skyscrapers in the city.

On the twenty-fifth anniversary of the crash, the *New York Times* ran an article including two interviews with survivors, one of whom was on the seventy-ninth floor and another, who by sheer fluke, had been called away just in the nick of time. Miss Catherine O'Connor, then secretary to the relief agency's director, Monsignor Patrick A. O'Boyle (now Patrick Cardinal O'Boyle of Washington, D.C.), and now retired said, "Do I remember?" She had been reading the morning mail and was walking across the office when she heard "a terrific explosion and the building rocking so," and then came "the burst of flames which consumed the office instantaneously." "We had no idea what had happened, but we were completely surrounded by flames and in pitch-black smoke."

"Believe it or not, we prayed," she recalled. "We knew this was the end, we knew there was no way out. You had strange thoughts, thoughts of many things, and prayed." Miss O'Connor, whose feet were burned by the heat of the floors, was taken to a hospital for treatment of the burns, for shock, and for smoke poisoning that she says has never entirely left her. In October she went back to work.

Mr. Edmund E. Cummings, still with the Catholic Relief Organization, had gone in early that morning to meet with another staff member, Jack McCloskey and Monsignor Edward E. Swanstrom, now Bishop Swanstrom. About 9:30 the monsignor called to tell him to meet instead in a barbershop nearby. Cummings and McCloskey "went downstairs and were just about to enter the barbershop when we heard the boom." Then they saw the orange flames and smoke and "began to worry about our own people." The three men walked back to the building and went up to the seventy-ninth floor, when the bishop administered the last rites. Cummings was asked to identify the dead.

"The plane went in where McCloskey and I were sitting," he said. "The only thing left of my desk were the metal fittings; the wooden desk was burned right down to the floor, and the tile of the floor," he recalled, "was also burned, exposing the concrete, and the bodies were also burned beyond recognition." Later, after a good stiff drink, Cummings went home. "In conversation, people mention the airplane that went into the Empire State. When they do, I reply I know all about it 'intimately.' But for the grace of God I wouldn't be here, for the bishop saved my life by calling me downstairs," he said.

One touch of macabre humor was registered that day. There was one employee in the building who was chronically late, and that Saturday he punched the time clock on the eighty-sixth floor at the exact instant the plane hit the building. The terrific noise so unnerved him that he raced down the stairs all the way to the lobby, in fact registering the fastest time ever recorded for the descent. When he reached the lobby he fell, and police picked him up, but his legs were still pedaling furiously. He couldn't stop. They finally quieted him down and asked what had happened. "I'd been warned about reporting late," he said shakily, "and when I punched the clock and heard the crash I thought somebody had booby-trapped it to teach me a lesson."

141

7

And to the Present

t took one year and over $1 million to repair the damage from the crash. And no sooner had the Empire State Building recovered from the collision than the elevator operators went out on strike. A group of businessmen who were holding a meeting on one of the upper floors ordered sandwiches and beverages from a sandwich shop down at street level. When the delivery man arrived they promptly tipped him $75. Another man waited three days in his office for "an important phone call," a call he did finally receive. However, the strike was soon settled and things got back to normal.

The Empire State Building and television have always been synonymous. Back in the early 1930s the Radio Corporation of America and the General Electric Company were granted permission from the Federal Communications Commission to jointly erect an experimental television station, in the metropolitan New York area, which would be operated by the National Broadcasting Company. Images of Mickey Mouse were successfully transmitted from the top of the tower. Then, in 1950, above the 102nd-floor-level observatory, as a result of three years of study and ex-

View north from the 102nd-floor observatory
The Hudson River is at lef

(*Above*) These workmen, in the process of building the Empire State Building's television tower in the early 1950s, were virtually standing atop New York City. (*Right*) A view of the master TV antenna

perimentation on a space the size of a pitcher's mound, a mastlike structure, 222 feet (22 stories) high and 60 tons in weight, was constructed stretching upward into the clouds to a height of 1,472 feet. It is still the world's most powerful and far-reaching TV tower. From here, nine of Greater New York's television stations transmit their programs throughout four states. Although now there are plans to move the TV transmitting equipment to the top of the World Trade Center, extensive experiments and testing are yet to determine whether or not this will become a reality.

Also located in the vicinity of the 102nd-floor level is the Empire State Building master FM antenna, the world's first such antenna, one that allows multiple stations to broadcast simultaneously. Installed in 1965, it can accommodate seventeen stations.

Early morning clean

In 1955, further recognition was bestowed upon the building by the American Society of Civil Engineers, who marked it as one of the seven wonders of American engineering. Others included were the Colorado River Aqueduct, Grand Coulee Dam and the Columbia Basin Project, Hoover Dam, the Panama Canal, the San Francisco-Oakland Bay Bridge and Chicago's sewage-disposal system. The following year, in 1956, a series of beacons were installed, called Freedom Lights. These could be seen for fifty miles, but were later dismantled.

Although the building has provided a rich flow of exciting news over the years, some new financial facts were added in September of 1961 that made real estate history. At that time it was announced that the building would be sold to a group of investors headed by Lawrence A. Wien, a New York attorney and realty investor. Associated with Wien was Harry B. Helmsley, whose reputation in real estate touches four bases: he is a leading broker, a major investor, president of Helmsley-Spear, Inc., one of the largest real estate management concerns in the world, and an investment builder. The building at the time was to be sold by Colonel Henry Crown, the Chicago industrialist who was originally part of a group that had bought the building from the John J. Raskob Estate in 1951 for $34 million. At the same time the land under the building was bought separately by the Prudential Insurance Company of America, for $17 million.

Negotiations to acquire the Empire State had started in 1954, with Harry B. Helmsley, as broker, quarterbacking the deal through 1959, 1960, and 1961. Under the terms of the agreement the Wien syndicate acquired complete control of the Empire State Building under a 114-year master lease from the Prudential Insurance Company. The insurance company, which already owned the land, simultaneously purchased the building from Colonel Crown, subject to the Wien master lease, as an investment for its 36 million policy holders. The purchase price of $65 million, averaging out to $6.50 a brick, was the highest ever paid for a single building, with the Wien interests contributing $36 million and Prudential $29 million.

The closing, held in December of 1961, was so complex that the thirty-four principal participants, seated around a thirty-seven-foot teakwood table in the board room of Prudential's headquarters in Newark, New Jersey, followed the proceedings with the help of a twenty-nine page agenda. That the transaction kept a battery of lawyers, accountants, tax experts, and title insurance companies hard at work is reflected in their handiwork, which consists of a contract of sale and exhibits that ran over four hundred pages, supplemented by another hundred legal documents. To minimize confusion, some of the participants conducted a series of "dress rehearsals" of the closing over the two-week period preceding the formal signing, an event that took over four hours to conclude.

Lawrence A. Wein created the huge transaction, and Harry B. Helmsley engineered it. Successful in their own specialized fields, together they privately developed one of the nation's largest real estate empires, owning and controlling large amounts of property from coast to coast. It is estimated that their mutual holdings have a value of over $1.5 billion dollars, aside from their other interests.

It should be added that the acquisition was financed by a unique vehicle, the raising of $33 million through a public syndication registered with both the Securities Exchange Commission and the attorney general of New York State. Empire State Building Associates was created by Wien, and under his direction and without the assistance of any outside underwriter, participations were sold in $5,000 and $10,000 units, the largest amount of cash ever raised through this type of financing.

In most real estate circles, it was felt that if anybody could raise over $30 million by the syndication route, it would be Wien. He had been a strong and successful proponent of this particular financing method, having raised well over $200 million through syndications since 1948. For Helmsley, his role as broker in the sale of the building was a crowning achievement in a star-studded career. As president of Helmsley-Spear, he

(Pages 149–152) In these photographs one can see tho
from the many neighborhoods of New York, the Empire State Buildin
is an ever-visible symbol of the majesty of the cit
Photos Elizabeth C. Bake

directs an operation that manages over two hundred office, loft, apartment and hotel properties in New York City, plus many others throughout the country. The properties his firm manages in New York alone are valued at more than $3 billion.

In acquiring control of the building, the Wien group took over management of the world-renowned center of business and industry. Today, its 2 million square feet of office space are shared by more than 900 firms from six continents; and no single tenant occupies as much as 10 percent of the building's total rentable area, a type of tenancy that the management prefers, in contrast to most of their counterparts, who eagerly seek full-floor or multifloor tenants.

Over the last twenty years the building has rung up an enviable renting record, with its occupancy level averaging over 95 percent, but what is more significant has been its ability to compete successfully with the scores of new buildings placed on the market since the end of the Second World War. Today its owners can point with pride to a building virtually fully rented, with no untenanted space exceeding 6,000 square feet.

More than anything else, perceptive ownership and enlightened management, augmented by an extensive program of modernization—a program accelerated with the Wien takeover late in 1961—have enabled the Empire State to keep its competitive edge.

The new management promptly brought to bear a vast fund of know-how with the appointment of Helmsley-Spear, Inc., as renting and managing agent. At that time, Helmsley named Robert L. Luery as general manager of the building, to handle all the operational aspects, including leasing and managing as well as modernization. Luery has since created his own real estate firm in Connecticut and has been succeeded as Empire State Building general manager by Robert L. Tinker, who had served as rental manager. Tinker has done an outstanding job in this most important assignment.

Despite the many changes undertaken by the new owners, they wisely retained one of the building's most vital links with its original inspiration.

He is H. Hamilton Weber, the man selected by John J. Raskob and Pierre S. du Pont, the original owners of the Empire State Building, to conceive and carry out all renting campaigns for the skyscraper. Formerly president of the National Association of Building Owners and Managers, Weber remains with the building as a consultant on tenant relations.

Shortly after Helmsley-Spear entered the picture, a multimillion-dollar program was initiated that affected practically every area of the building, both public and private, inside and out. The cathedral-like lobby, adorned by a profusion of marble imported from four countries, was air conditioned and given a new lighting system, along with spectacular, illuminated depictions of the Eight Wonders of the World. The building itself is one of them. The others are: The Great Pyramids, the Hanging Gardens of Babylon, the Statue of Zeus, the Temple of Diana, the Lighthouse of Pharos, the Colossus of Rhodes, and the Tomb of King Mausolus.

Two sets of moving stairways were installed to transport people down to the Concourse, where there is a new observatory ticket office, and up to the second floor, where a number of banks and brokerage offices are located. The two observatories, focal points of all tourist activity, have been given a new flavor with a wholesale refurbishing. A unique display by many of New York's leading educational and cultural institutions has been created on the second floor. The building's entire limestone façade has been cleaned and painted, and electrical systems and corridor lighting improved. A new freight-loading platform has increased shipping and delivery capacity by 25 percent.

The building has been given a modern system of central air conditioning, climate control to assure year-round comfort in all office areas and public spaces, with engineers keeping a twenty-four-hour vigil to insure a complete change of air twelve times each hour. Modern illumination is provided by fluorescent lighting, recessed in dropped, acoustical ceilings, which are still noticeably higher than ceilings in newer buildings.

The main lobby from inside the Fifth Avenue doors, looking toward the Information Desk

The automation of fifty-eight passenger elevators was the largest single job of its kind on record, and had to be done in stages in order to avoid disrupting the normally heavy building traffic. This project involved 7 miles of shafts containing 9 million feet of insulated wire, 250,000 feet of conduit, almost 30 miles of rail, and 120 miles of wire rope.

The project created several unusual problems. First, there was the matter of automating a few elevators at a time in each bank and still keeping the others running efficiently. Once these adjustments were made, special electronic equipment had to be designed and installed to allow the newly automated cars to coordinate their traffic patterns with those of the cars still being modernized.

Every wire and connection was preengineered, and made in accordance with a two-year master installation plan. All of the installed electronic and computer equipment was custom designed and built to fit into the space allocated in the motor rooms, where, because of the limited space, a second tier had to be constructed to accommodate the new apparatus.

The automated system utilizes supervisor-demand programmed electronic computer techniques, which constantly scan traffic needs and instantaneously dispatch elevators to meet the varying demand. It has been reported that the new system is at least 30 to 35 percent more efficient than the manual operation.

Working hand in hand with elevator technicians were the marble men, who removed and put up new marble and cut out openings in the marble walls to accommodate the new cabs. They literally had to uncover walls for the elevator cars and then reconstruct them block by block. They likewise put up new marble facing for the escalator areas and have also done a lot of marble, stone, and granite work for individual tenants.

The monumental exterior scrubbing job, which was carried out in stages over a six-month period, involved cleaning, coating, and touching up 500,000 square feet of limestone along the quarter-mile sides of the building by a crew of 30 men using electric climbing scaffolds. Twenty cables, each 1,200 feet long, were used to suspend the electricity-driven

The main lobby of the Empire State Building revealing the new marble facing

THE GREAT PYRAMIDS	HANGING GARDENS OF BABYLON

Oldest of the Seven Wonders of the Ancient World is Egypt's Great Cheops pyramid at Giza, built about 5,000 years ago and still standing. This awesome mass of stone blocks, covering thirteen acres and high as a forty-story building, took 100,000 slaves and more than twenty years of hand labor to build. Adjacent are two slightly smaller pyramids, tombs of the succeeding pharaohs, Chephren, and Mycerinus. The Sphinx portrays the pharaoh, Chephren, with the body of a crouching lion.

Nebuchadnezzar, King of Babylon (600 B.C.) was said to have built the Hanging Gardens for his wife, Amytis, because she was homesick for the flowers and trees around her former home in Media. The Gardens consisted of an immense successive setback of terraces 30 stories high, each overflowing with spectacular masses of colorful blossoms and greenery, watered by a sprinkling system from the Euphrates River. Here, in beautiful apartments within the terraces, Nebuchadnezzar and his queen spent the rest of their days.

(Pages 158–161) The eight massive, illuminated panels by artist Roy Sparki⟨ give viewers a three-dimensional picture, in color, of the Ancient World's Seven Wonder⟨ and the Modern World's new Eighth Wonder—the Empire State Building

STATUE OF ZEUS

One of the early Seven Wonders of the World was this giant figure of Zeus seated in patriarchal majesty in the temple at Olympia. As the supreme god in Greek religion, Zeus had the attributes of thunder and lightning to exercise his authority. His forty-foot high statue by Phidias, considered to be the greatest artist of ancient Greece (c. 500–432 B.C.), was carved from ivory, while the hair, beard, and garments were made of gold, and the eyes of precious jewels.

TEMPLE OF DIANA

Dominating the vast and somber interior of the temple bearing her name was this huge statue of Diana, goddess of nature and of women in childbirth. To this famous shrine were attracted more travelers than any other building in ancient history. It was here that Paul the Apostle challenged pagan worship and enraged the crowd. Built about 350 B.C. at Ephesus, this magnificent temple was despoiled by Nero in A.D. 67 and destroyed by the barbarian Goths in A.D. 260.

159

LIGHTHOUSE OF PHAROS

Considered to be the greatest lighthouse ever built, this forerunner to modern skyscrapers was erected about 200 B.C. by Ptolemy Philadelphus on the island of Pharos near Alexandria. Built entirely of marble (steel girders were then unknown), the Lighthouse of Pharos rose 600 feet high and housed a military barracks and many offices. It lasted for over a thousand years and was destroyed by an earthquake in A.D. 1375.

COLOSSUS OF RHODES

To commemorate their heroic defense against attacking Macedonians and as a warning to future invaders, the Rhodians erected this awe-inspiring image of Helios, the Sun God, in the harbor of the Greek island of Rhodes about 280 B.C. Cast of bronze melted from the war machines left behind by the defeated Macedonians, the great statue towered to an overall height of 160 feet. It was toppled by an earthquake in 224 B.C.

TOMB OF KING MAUSOLUS

Inspired by a consuming grief, the widowed
Queen Artemisia raised this stately monument
at Halicarnassus in memory of King Mausolus,
who ruled Caria from 387 to 353 B.C. Wishing
her husband's name to endure through the
ages, Artemisia commissioned the most gifted
artists and architects to create his tomb.
Richly wrought with gold and sculptural orna-
mentation, the marble masterpiece became one
of the Seven Wonders of the World and
added the word "mausoleum" to our lan-
guage, thus achieving Artemisia's wish for her
husband's immortality.

THE 8TH WONDER OF THE WORLD

The tallest and most famous building of all
time—the Empire State Building. This triumph
of architectural and engineering genius—the
Eighth Wonder of the World—soars 1,472 feet
into the sky—as high as all the original Seven
Wonders piled one on top of the other. A
city in itself—virtually a city of marvels—the
Empire State Building has a population of
16,000 persons working in the building plus
35,000 visitors daily—totaling more visitors
in a single year than the combined totals of
all who visited the original Seven Wonders
of the World.

scaffolds. Because of the building's great height, the scaffolds climbed up and down the cables, which were suspended at their full length throughout the operation.

Starting at the 86th floor, specially rigged baskets carried crews to the 102nd floor, where they worked on the cylindrical face of the tower at that level. To restore the original limestone color and eliminate carbon stains took a record amount of waterproof coating—3,000 gallons.

Besides scrubbing, it was necessary to clean the metal frames of windows with wire brushes, apply rust-inhibitor paint and coat the frames with lead-and-oil paint. That job alone required 2,500 gallons of special paint. It is believed to be the largest exterior paint-coating contract ever awarded for a single building.

Metal cleaners and solvents were used to restore the natural brilliance of the eight-inch-wide stainless-steel strips that run the height of the building. The job also included repointing all defective mortar joints in the limestone with an elastic compound, as well as window perimeters and the spandrel joints around the ornamental steel strips.

Another job that required several months to complete was reroofing the setback terraces, which had been finished with red quarry tile when the building was opened. The tile was replaced with a more modern-looking topping consisting of white chip slag applied over a rigid four-ply insulation board. Cant strip flashings were installed against all parapet walls, and in certain locations, where the roof meets the wall, asbestos felt was applied to assure continuous drainage. Approximately 65,000 square feet of setback area were reroofed, and about half a mile of flashing installed, all with a minimum of inconvenience to tenants, although materials and workmen often had to move through occupied space to get to the setbacks.

Keeping the world's tallest office building looking immaculate from top to bottom is the daily chore of some 200 employees. Each twenty-four-hour period, the crew travels through the building, cleaning the 1.8 million square feet of office space, another 280,000 square feet of public corridors, 37,999 square feet of lavatories, the elevators, and 270 stairways between the floors. To indicate the magnitude of their task, each month over 2,000 chemically treated dustcloths are used, along with 250 gallons of wax, 150 gallons of all-purpose cleaner, and 500 pounds of conventional cleaning cloths.

Whereas all interior space is maintained on a twenty-four-hour-a-day basis, the building's 6,500 windows are washed monthly. The job is unique because of the demands made upon the contractor by the regularly assigned crew, who actually qualify for "combat pay" as a result of their efforts hundreds of feet above New York's streets. The company has developed an unusual method of cleaning the structure's windows on the upper floors, where on gusty days the wind blows up, not down. As a result, the men have had to "reverse their field" and clean the bottom section of each window pane first and then the upper part, and move up from floor to floor.

Because the Empire State Building is one of the world's largest commercial office structures, it generates more waste material daily than most other buildings do in a week. The problem of removing the tons of paper and trash accumulated each day has been resolved scientifically and mechanically. The operation begins shortly after six o'clock each night, when the corps of cleaning women who invade the offices start dumping the contents of the waste baskets in fifty-pound canvas bags. These are taken by porters to the service elevators and down to a sprinklered room, where they are kept for twenty-four hours in case a tenant has mistakenly discarded valuable papers and wants to search through the waste to find them.

At 9:30 P.M., the porters start emptying sacks and the trash is transported to an automatic sixty-upstroke baling machine. When a thousand pounds are in the machine, an electric eye cuts off the bale and it is tied with wire. A tow motor pulls the bale to the loading platform, from

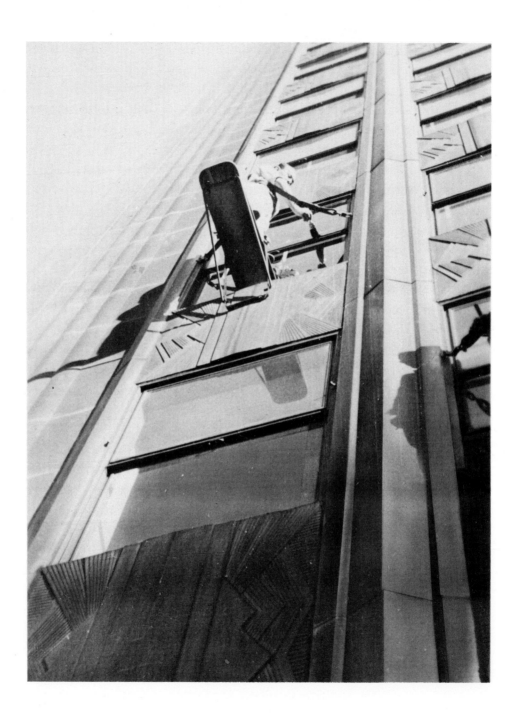

164

A window washer spruces up the building
Note the Art Deco detail on the plates between
the windows of each floor. *UPA*

whence it is carried away by a trailer truck. Waste removal averages 130 tons a month, the contractor reports.

A final maintenance note: Thirst must be slaked, and the office water cooler is as much a gathering place in the Empire State Building as in other offices. Tens of thousands of five-gallon bottles of water and 2.5 million paper cups are used annually by the building's tenants. A full-time man is on hand during office hours just to service Empire State tenants, and to supervise the distribution of the water.

Probably the most spectacular of the recent improvements was the sky-hung "chandelier," the result of floodlighting the top thirty floors of the tower. The new illumination, which replaced the old beacons that used to sweep the sky, transformed the building into a nighttime landmark, one that airline pilots pointed out to travelers arriving after dark. It was turned on in April 1964 to coincide with the opening of the New York World's Fair. During the recent energy crisis the lights were extinguished, but once again, in honor of the nation's bicentennial, they light up the sky over Manhattan.

As part of the new management's reorganization program, five departments were created, to direct renting, building operation, observatory, construction, alteration and interior painting, and electronics and engineering. A first step was to centralize all these departments in one area, simultaneously laying the groundwork for a streamlined system of inter-office communication and releasing space for rental.

After reorganizing the Empire State Building's own table of organization and streamlining standard operating procedures, the new management then turned to the problem of trying to satisfy the growing pains of companies in the building. On several occasions Empire State management was approached by potential large space users who found that the building could not accommodate them. For a long time the building had little upper floor space for rent; in fact, the structure has had the enviable reputation of being virtually fully rented, except for some fractional space.

Although it was difficult to find substantial space for companies seeking to move into the building, it was even more urgent in the eyes of management that the huge structure not lose any existing tenants, many of whom have been in Empire State since it opened. Eventually, a top-to-bottom inspection tour of the skyscraper uncovered two fertile fields of rentable space on the lower levels, where much space was being wasted by the dispersal of so much machinery and storage facilities. In a series of conferences, the brass mapped a plan to consolidate most of the storage and machine shops in 25,000 square feet of space in a corner of what is now the Concourse and Lower Lobby. That section is, of course, screened from public view. The final plan permitted the Empire State to recapture approximately 75,000 square feet of space, 50,000 in the Lower Lobby and 25,000 on the Concourse, all of it now rented.

That there was rentable space to be gleaned on the two lower levels was at least an established, if not cultivated, fact. The floor directly below the main lobby, now known as the Concourse, represents the culmination of an idea originally drafted by the building's architects back in the late 1920s. Their objective was only partially carried out: a public arcade was begun on this level but left unfinished when the building opened on May 1, 1931. It is said that the plan was abandoned because the building's sponsors felt that with the depression taking its toll of business, there would be enough of a problem renting office space above ground.

As a result of the abandoned work, the level retained a surrealistic "ghost town" quality for thirty-six years. The eighteen-foot-high corridors that would have formed the arcade were dim and eerie, an effect further heightened by partially completed storefronts and many doors that didn't open. The space of these halls was often either left unused or utilized for storage by the companies that rented main lobby space above.

The Concourse project is only half the story. Directly below that level

166

is the Lower Lobby, as it is presently identified, and like its upstairs cousin formerly an area reserved for storage, warehouse facilities, and building service equipment. It is today a focal point of business activity.

The blueprint called for conversion of the Lower Lobby first, a procedure that created 50,000 square feet of rentable space. It has become a microcosm of the computer industry; included in one tenant's space are a 200-seat auditorium and a specially air-conditioned computer room with its own "floating" floor.

Besides the four high-speed passenger elevators, there are two marble grand staircases, installed as part of the original arcade concept on the north and south sides of the lobby, that provide access to the Concourse. The travertine floors and stainless-steel handrails on the staircases have been preserved, and the temporary walls erected in the 1930s at the halfway landings have been removed.

One key feature of the management's modus operandi is to cooperate closely with outside leasing brokers. The establishment of the National Notions Mart on the twelfth, thirteenth, and fourteenth floors is a case in point. In 1963 Jerome M. Cohen, then a vice-president of Williams & Company, and now president, approached Helmsley-Spear with the suggestion that a block of space in the building be set aside for rental to firms in the notions industry, which had been experiencing a tremendous growth.

Many of the industry's major companies were occupying space in the neighborhood but were seeking new quarters, and as a convenience to buyers, preferably in a building that could house all their respective operations. One of the prerequisites of a new center, however, was a prestige address. The National Notions Mart was created, and through the collaborative efforts of brokers, notions firms occupy approximately 70,000 square feet in the building.

The Notions Mart is only one of several industries headquartered at the Empire State Building. In recent years the building has become the base of operations for more than 109 companies in the shoe industry and another 100 companies in the shirt and hosiery fields. The building, in effect, is a thriving commercial base for nearly 1,000 national and international businesses, constituting a tenant roster unique not only numerically but qualitatively as well. The banking fraternity is represented by such giants as Bankers Trust, Irving Trust, and Manufacturers Hanover Trust, all of which maintain branch offices in the building. American industry is represented by the Seagrave Corporation, Dow Badische, E. I. du Pont de Nemours, U.S. Industries, Kayser-Roth Shoes, the Rexham Corporation, Jockey International, Blue Bell, and the B.V.D. Company. Diversification of tenancy is exemplified by such companies as Publix Shirt, Maro Industries, International Shoe, Trans International Airlines, Western International Hotels, the California Wine Association, the Gibralter Factors Corporation, the Cigar Manufacturers Association, the Lark Luggage Corporation, Genesco, and Wagner, Quillinan & Tennant (the law firm of former New York City mayor Robert F. Wagner and of Francis E. Quillinan, son-in-law of the late Alfred E. Smith).

Being the most famous building in the world, there is an international flavor arising from the wide variety of tenants who either are of foreign origin or who do business with countries or firms outside the United States. To name a few there are the Japan Pulp and Paper (U.S.A.) Corporation, the Korean Trade Promotion Center, the Helm New York Chemical Corporation, Fuji Photo Film U.S.A., Impex Overseas, Asahi Chemical Industry America, Iran Foundation, Chori America, Quasar TV and Kanebo U.S.A.

Virtually all of the Empire State Building is "shallow space" with an unusually high proportion of window area, ideal for smaller tenants with a high percentage of executive space requirements. Furthermore, occupancy by a diversified tenancy is preferred, it is explained, because it actually enables the owner to develop a much more stable financial picture. No single tenant dominates the rent roll. If a large amount of space is divided into comparatively smaller units, the owners can derive more income than if the same space were taken by a full floor user, even though the rate schedule is competitive with other buildings in Manhattan. Also, the difficulty of meeting the demands that exceptionally large tenants sometimes make is avoided. Obviously, this approach has been proved successful. An analysis of the tenant roster, checked by computer, indicates that the majority of the Empire State tenants have occupied space in the building for an average of ten years.

There are several reasons why the Empire State can still give its newest competitors a run for their money. It has the intangible asset of prestige, enabling it to draw tenants from all over the world. The building's eminence is best reflected in the fact that it had no formal address until many years after it was completed. At the insistence of postal authorities, it was finally listed as 350 Fifth Avenue, but most mail is still addressed only as Empire State Building, New York City.

As for landmark visitors, the 4 millionth visitor was actor Jimmy Stewart back on March 28, 1940. In May 1961 Herta Steffans, eighteen, of Germany was the 20 millionth visitor, and in May of 1971 the 40 millionth visitor arrived. Mrs. Joseph O. Boeglin of Anderson, Indiana, was waiting in line to go to the top. The ticket seller in the Concourse advised her that there was no visibility up top, but she insisted that she had come all the way from Indiana and wouldn't miss a trip to the top for the world. She bought her ticket and was then informed that she was a milestone visitor. After visiting the top she was the guest of honor at a reception held in the eighty-sixth-floor observatory and received a number of mementos, including a sterling silver lifetime pass to the observatory, a silver model of the building, tickets for a Pan Am World Airways flight to Bermuda and a week's stay at the Inverurie Hotel.

Finally, it can be said that the Empire State Building is more than just another very tall manmade structure. Those who conceived it, those who designed it, those who built it, and those who are now charged with managing it, have all brought to its heart of steel and stone a very special personality. Despite the very grand schemes for other buildings, it is undoubtedly certain that none will ever match its flawless lines or rival its startling beauty. And in the final analysis, none can ever capture the imagination of the entire world as has the Empire State Building.

Appendix: Interesting Facts

LOCATION

350 Fifth Avenue, between 33rd and 34th Street, New York, N. Y. 10001

ARCHITECTS

Shreve, Lamb & Harmon Associates, 475 Park Avenue South, New York, N. Y. 10016

BUILDERS

Starrett Brothers & Eken, Inc., 301 East 57th Street, New York, N. Y. 10022

MANAGING AGENTS

Helmsley-Spear, Inc., 60 East 42nd Street, New York, N. Y. 10017

HEIGHT

1,472 feet (448 meters) to top of TV tower
1,250 feet (391 meters) to 102nd-floor observatory
1,050 feet (320 meters) to 86th-floor observatory

WEIGHT

365,000 tons (14 tons to support each occupant)

VOLUME

37 million cubic feet

AREA OF SITE

83,860 square feet (about 2 acres)

BASEMENT AND LOWER LOBBY

35 feet below ground

COST INCLUDING LAND

$40,948,900

COST OF BUILDING ALONE

$24,718,000 (expected cost of $50 million did not materialize due to the Great Depression)

CONSTRUCTION SCHEDULE

Excavation: Begun January 22, 1930, before demolition of old Waldorf-Astoria Hotel on the site had ended

Construction: Begun on March 17, 1930. Framework rose at the rate of 4½ stories per week

Cornerstone: Laid by Alfred E. Smith, former governor of New York, on September 17, 1930

Masonry completed: November 13, 1930

Official opening: May 1, 1931, by President Herbert Hoover, who pressed a button in Washington, D.C., to turn on the building's lights

Total time: 7 million man-hours, 1 year and 45 days work, including Sundays and holidays

Work force: 3,400 during peak periods

BUILDING MATERIALS

Exterior: Indiana limestone and granite, trimmed with aluminum and chrome-nickel-steel from the 6th floor to the top

Lobby: Ceiling-high marble, imported from France, Italy, Belgium, and Germany

STRUCTURAL STATISTICS

Bricks: 10 million

Electrical wire: 2,500,000 feet

Fire hose connections: 400

Outer walls: 730 tons of aluminum and stainless steel

Radiator pipe: 50 miles

Steel frame: 60,000 tons (sufficient to build a double-track railroad from New York to Baltimore)

Steps: 1,860 from street level to 102nd floor

Stone: 200,000 cubic feet

Telephone and telegraph cable: 3,500 miles

Telephones in building: 18,000

Water pipe: 70 miles

Windows: 6,500

FACILITIES AND SERVICES

Air conditioning: The Empire State Building is cooled by 5,250 tons of refrigeration equipment located below ground. The equipment is operated by 460-volt, 60-cycle, three-phase electric current. Cooling towers, consisting of six cells, are located on the Thirty-third Street side of the building, above the off-street loading platforms.

Distribution of chilled water is accomplished through extra-heavy pipes of various sizes, up to 14 inches in diameter. Some 500 air-handling units, pneumatically controlled and completely automatic, are strategically located in the building. They help effect a complete change of air 6 times each hour. This system is used to provide winter ventilation by circulating warm water in the cool period of the year. The installation of air-conditioning was begun in 1950.

Electricity usage: Approximately 35 million Kilowatt hours every year. Normally, electric power for buildings comes from underground wiring and transformers. At the Empire State a vertical distribution network is used, requiring vaults of transformers at various levels, including two at the 84th floor, which houses the highest transformer vault in any building in the world.

Elevators: There are a total of 73 elevators in the Empire State Building, including 6 freight elevators. The elevators, operating at speeds ranging from 600 to 1,200 feet a minute, are enclosed in 7 miles of elevator shaft. A passenger can reach the eightieth floor of the building in one minute. The Empire State, with more elevators than any other building in New York, offers service on a 24-hour basis.

Moving Stairways: Nine high-speed moving stairways serve the building's Concourse, Lower Lobby, and lobby and second-floor areas.

Water System: At the Empire State Building, two water systems, each with its own pumping, storage, and distribution equipment, accommodate the needs of tenants and occupants. One is a sanitary water system for drinking and other personal uses; the other is for fire protection. The sanitary water system can be diverted to fire use, if needed.

Most pumps for both systems are located below ground. Water tanks are located within the building as follows:

101st floor (5,000 gallons) ; gravity feeds all lower floors to the 85th
85th floor (12,000 gallons) ; gravity feeds all lower floors to the 63rd
63rd floor (12,000 gallons) ; gravity feeds all lower floors to the 46th
46th floor (5,000 gallons) ; gravity feeds all lower floors to the 31st
31st floor (5,000 gallons) ; gravity feeds all lower floors to the 21st
21st floor (20,000 gallons) ; gravity feeds all lower floors to the street level

Auxiliary fire tanks are located on various other floors. Hot water is obtained by heating by steam.

Water Consumption: 26,500 cubic feet daily. Record set in August 1959, 52,200 cubic feet

Bibliography

American Weekly, March 18, 1962.

Architectural Forum, many editions.

Bailey, Vernon H. *Empire State, A Pictorial Record of Its Construction*. New York: W. E. Rudge, 1931.

"Empire State Building." *Real Estate Forum*, Nov. 14, 1971.

The Empire State Building Official Souvenir Book.

Haskell, D. "A Temple of Jehu." *The Nation*, May 27, 1931.

James, Theodore, Jr. *Fifth Avenue*. New York: Walker & Co., 1971.

Low, Francis. "A Chase Up Into the Sky." *American Heritage Magazine*.

"Man's Mightiest Monument: Empire State Building, New York." *Popular Mechanics*, December 1930.

Nash, Ogden. "Atop the Mooring Mast." *The New Yorker*, March 21, 1931.

New York Herald-Tribune, many editions.

New York Sun, many editions.

The New York Times, many editions.

New York World-Telegram, many editions.

"Sky Boys Who Rode the Ball on the Empire State." *Literary Digest*, May 23, 1931.

Wilson, E. "Progress and Poverty: Empire State Building." *The New Republic*, May 20, 1931.

Index

179

DATE DUE

GAYLORD		PRINTED IN U.S.A.